SAGE INSTANT ACCOUNTING

in easy steps

Bill Mantovani

COMPUTER
STEP

In easy steps is an imprint of Computer Step
Southfield Road . Southam
Warwickshire CV33 OFB . England

Tel: 01926 817999 Fax: 01926 817005
http://www.computerstep.com

Notice of Liability
Every effort has been made to ensure that this book contains accurate
and current information. However, Computer Step and the author shall
not be liable for any loss or damage suffered by readers as a result of
any information contained herein.

Trademarks
Microsoft® and Windows® are registered trademarks of Microsoft
Corporation. Sage Instant® is a registered trademark of The Sage
Group Plc. All other trademarks are acknowledged as belonging to
their respective companies.

Printed and bound in the United Kingdom

ISBN 1-84078-003-7

Contents

5   The Nominal Ledger   53

6   The Bank   69

7   Products   85

Installing Instant Accounting

This chapter is for those who are installing Sage Instant Accounting 2000 for the first time or upgrading from an earlier version. It gives you the minimum system requirements, shows you how to perform the installation or upgrade and introduces you to the features and improvements of the latest version.

Covers

Chapter One

Introduction

We all know how important it is for businesses to keep accurate records of their accounts. With a computerised accounting system, it is equally important to ensure that the right details are used because if the information is not entered correctly, then the accounts could still be wrong. After all, it's easy to blame the computer!

Accuracy reduces errors and prevents costly mistakes.

This book introduces you to Sage Instant Accounting and takes you through, step by step, the various options provided within the program for keeping your business finances completely up to date. Of course it is up to you, the user, to make sure that information is entered regularly and this book teaches you how and when.

Preparing to Install Sage Instant Accounting

Before you can start using Sage Instant Accounting you need to install the program onto your computer. If you are already using an older version of Instant Accounting and wish to upgrade to the latest version, this is explained later in this chapter.

ScanDisk and Disk Defragmenter can be found by clicking on Start, Programs, Accessories and System Tools. Alternatively, you can also access these utilities from the Windows desktop by first double-clicking on My Computer then clicking on the Drive C: icon with the right mouse button, selecting Properties, then the Tools tab.

For all programs to run correctly on a computer it is important that the computer system itself is working correctly. This is, therefore, the perfect time to run certain 'housekeeping' functions on your PC to ensure no faults have crept into the system, particularly hard disk errors. Windows 95/98 and NT/2000 come complete with disk diagnostic routines which you should run regularly anyway, so before starting the installation of Sage Instant Accounting work through this checklist:

- Delete any unnecessary files, such as from the Temp folder.

- Make sure the Recycle Bin is empty.

- Run ScanDisk to check for, and correct, any hard disk errors.

- Run the Disk Defragmenter utility to tidy up the hard disk.

Features and Improvements

 Use the new Task Manager for setting up a reminder list of things to do every time you start your computer.

Sage Instant Accounting lets you manage and control your business finances easily and quickly. For existing users, the latest version incorporates a number of new or improved features to help you process your accounts even easier. For Instant Accounting 2000 these include:

New Features

- A new Welcome Screen, from where you can launch Instant Accounting 2000, Task Manager, Help and access the Internet.

- A Late Payments facility.

- The VAT Transfer Wizard.

- Streamlined Bank Routines, including grouping on receipts and reconciliation routines, a search facility within the Bank option and improved payments option.

- New Reports, including the Departmental Analysis (Totals) and the Product List by Category reports.

- A new Find option in the Error Correction facility.

- On-line capabilities to support e-mail and web access.

 Use the VAT Transfer Wizard to transfer money from the Sales and Purchase Tax Control accounts to the VAT Liability account.

Improved Features

- Easier Installation procedure.

- Improved Wizards, including the Easy Startup Wizard to make it easier to set up your new company.

- An improved Balance Sheet report, including a new Long Term Liabilities section.

- Improved Credit Management displaying Account Status and telephone tips for chasing debt.

- Updated demonstration data or 'trial company' records to help you familiarise yourself with the various routines without using your own accounts.

 Use the Open Demo Data facility from the File menu to practice on demonstration data without danger of making a mistake on your own company data. To get back to your company data when you have finished practising, select Open Instant Data from the File menu.

System Requirements

If you want to make use of the Internet facilities your computer must have a live connection to the Internet.

Sage Instant Accounting is a single user, single company program that will work on a variety of hardware configurations, provided the minimum requirements are met. The latest version, Sage Instant Accounting 2000, is Year 2000 compliant, which means that it will not be affected by dates prior to, during and after the year 2000.

Before installing Instant Accounting you should first check that your computer system has the following recommended requirements for your new Sage program:

Make sure your computer system is fully Year 2000 compliant if you want to avoid possible problems in the future. Programs to test and fix your computer hardware are readily available either from suppliers or on the internet.

- An IBM compatible Pentium 90 or greater running one of the operating systems detailed below.

- At least 16Mb of RAM memory.

- At least 40Mb of free hard disk space after Windows has been installed.

- A SVGA or higher resolution video card and monitor supported by Windows.

- A Windows supported printer.

- A Microsoft compatible mouse.

It is also recommended that you have one of the following operating systems installed on your computer:

- Microsoft Windows 98.

- Windows 95.

- Windows NT Workstation V4 (or higher).

- Windows v3.1 or higher.

- Windows for Workgroups v3.11.

To find out more about upgrading a PC or the Year 2000 problem refer to the Upgrading Your PC and Year 2000 books in the 'in easy steps' series.

Should your computer system not meet the above recommended requirements you will need to enquire about an upgrade from your supplier. Also, although Instant Accounting is Year 2000 compliant you must not forget to check that your hardware is Year 2000 compliant as well.

Installing Instant Accounting for the first time

Exit all Windows programs before running the Instant Accounting installation program.

If you are using Windows 3.1 or 3.11, from the Program Manager menu bar choose File for Step 1.

If you are installing from floppy disk, insert disk 1 and type a:\setup for Step 3. Insert the next disk when prompted.

To prepare to upgrade from a previous version of Instant Accounting refer to page 14.

It is a relatively straight forward process to install Sage Instant Accounting, though you must remember to first ensure there are no Windows programs running before you do so. To install Instant Accounting 2000 for the first time do the following:

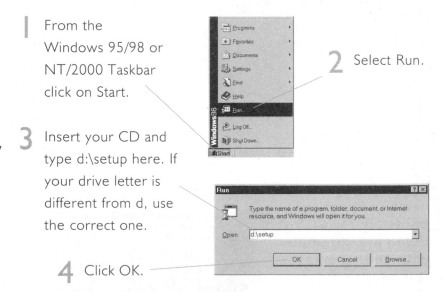

1 From the Windows 95/98 or NT/2000 Taskbar click on Start.

2 Select Run.

3 Insert your CD and type d:\setup here. If your drive letter is different from d, use the correct one.

4 Click OK.

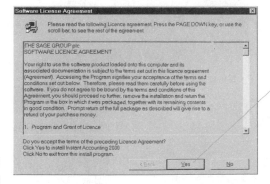

5 Choose Yes to agree to the terms and conditions of the Software Licence Agreement.

6 Click Next on the Welcome screen to continue with the installation, or Cancel to quit Setup.

If you make a mistake and wish to go back a step, simply click on the Back button.

7 To accept the default destination folder, click Next; otherwise, use Browse to change the destination before clicking Next.

8 In the Select Desktop Folder window, click Next to accept Sage as the default folder to install Instant Accounting into.

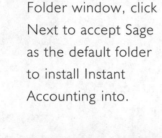

You can choose any Destination Folder name or Program Folder you wish, but if you are unfamiliar with your computer it is best to accept the Sage defaults.

9 You are now ready to install Instant Accounting. Check your selection and click Next to start the installation.

Should you decide to abort the installation for any reason, just click the Cancel button on any of the windows.

10 As Instant Accounting installs, an indicator shows the progress.

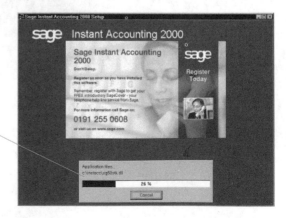

...cont'd

If you are using Windows 3.1 or 3.11, a new program group called Sage appears in your Program Manager window.

11 A new program group window called Sage appears. When necessary, close the window by clicking here.

The new program group will only be called Sage if you accepted the default name. If you changed the name in Step 8, the new program group will be called by whatever name you typed in.

12 When setup is complete, view the Readme file by ticking here and clicking Finish.

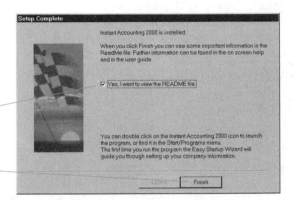

13 Click here to print the file so you can read it later.

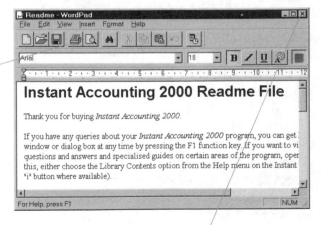

If you need to access the Readme file at a later date just click on Start, select Programs, Sage, then click on Sage Instant Accounting 2000 Readme.

14 To close the window click here.

Instant Accounting is now installed and ready to use for the first time.

Preparing to Upgrade to Accounting 2000

If you are upgrading from Instant v3.xx you will need to make a note of your customer statement defaults. To find this, open the Defaults menu, choose Customer Defaults, then choose the Statements tab.

Upgrading to Instant Accounting 2000 is easy, but the procedure is slightly different depending upon which version you are upgrading from. In all cases, though, you first need to prepare to upgrade by following these steps:

1 Find your existing program version number, e.g., Instant 97 v4.0, and note it down.

2 Note down the directory name where your existing program is stored, i.e.,c:\instacc.

3 Run your existing Instant Accounting program.

4 From the menu bar, click on File and Maintenance.

5 From the File maintenance window, click Check Data. Correct any errors.

Instant v3.xx users only – you cannot convert Statements, Remittance Advice, Letters and Labels stationery layouts to your new program. These will be overwritten with new default layouts. Therefore, you need to take a printout of these layouts if you want to change them in your new program.

6 Make a full backup of your Instant Accounting files from within your existing program. You are now ready to upgrade to your new program.

To prepare to upgrade from Instant v2.xx
As well as the above procedure, also do the following:

1 Check you have at least three times as much disk space free as your current data files occupy.

2 Compress your data files to remove any deleted data.

3 Take a printout of any amended or created stationery layouts.

4 Make a note of your password and any Criteria set up in your old program.

Upgrading to Sage Instant Accounting 2000

 Exit all Windows programs before you run the installation program.

 When upgrading from Instant Accounting v2.xx you must install into a new folder so you don't overwrite the existing installation.

 If you are using Windows 3.1 or 3.11, from the Program Manager menu bar choose File for Step 1.

 If you are installing from floppy disk, insert disk 1 and type a:\setup for Step 3. Insert the next disk when prompted.

Upgrading to Instant Accounting 2000 is very similar to installing it for the first time but with important differences depending on which version you are upgrading from, so follow these steps carefully:

1 From the Windows 95/98 or NT/2000 Taskbar click on Start.

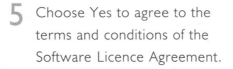

2 Select Run.

3 Insert your CD and type d:\setup here. If your drive letter is different from d, use the correct one.

4 Click OK.

5 Choose Yes to agree to the terms and conditions of the Software Licence Agreement.

6 On the Welcome screen click Next to continue.

7 In the Select folder window select the same folder as your current program if upgrading from Instant Accounting 97, 98 or v3.xx. If upgrading from v2.xx you must install into a new folder. Click Next.

8 Follow the on-screen instructions to complete the installation.

9 If asked whether you want to overwrite your existing stationery layouts, choose Yes or No as appropriate.

When finished, you are ready to convert your data files.

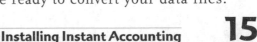

Converting your Data files

 If you are using Windows 3.1 or 3.11, from the Program Manager simply open the Sage group for Steps 1 and 2.

If you have upgraded from Instant Accounting v2.xx you will need to convert your old data files before you can use them. Simply do the following:

1 From the Windows 95/98 or NT/2000 Taskbar, click on Start.

2 Select Programs, then the Sage group.

3 Click on the Instant Accounting 2000 icon.

4 The Startup Wizard Appears.

 Your Serial Number and Activation Key are located on the inside front cover of your User's Guide.

5 Enter your Serial Number and Activation Key here.

6 Click Next.

 You can also overwrite your current Instant Accounting 2000 data using the Convert Data option from the Tools menu. When the Upgrade Data Wizard appears enter the drive and directory name of your old Sage program, choose Next to continue and follow the on-screen instructions.

7 Select the 'Upgrade data files from an earlier version' option.

8 Click Next and follow the on-screen instructions to complete the Startup Wizard.

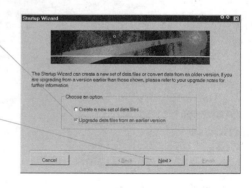

When the conversion of your data files is complete, your upgraded program is ready to use. If you make a mistake when you start to use your new program and before you have had the opportunity to make a backup, you can use the Convert Data option to overwrite your current Instant Accounting 2000 data with a fresh copy of your converted data files.

Getting Started

This chapter takes you through the stages of preparing Sage Instant Accounting for use. It explains initial procedures for setting up defaults required by the program.

Covers

Chapter Two

Introducing Sage Instant Accounting

Accuracy reduces errors and prevents costly mistakes.

All businesses need to keep accurate records of their accounts, and that is precisely what Instant Accounting helps you do. With it, you can record, control and examine your finances quickly and easily and see exactly where your money is coming from or going to.

Working through Sage Instant Accounting in easy steps

This book explains how to perform the main tasks required for keeping computerised business accounts. In the following chapters you are shown how to:

If Instant Accounting 2000 has been installed for the first time or you have upgraded from v2.xx, the installation wizard will place it in a folder called 'instacc'. If you are upgrading from other versions, the program is placed in the original Instant Accounting folder.

- Set defaults and Company preferences.

- Create customer and supplier records.

- Set up opening balances, maintain Bank accounts.

- Maintain the Nominal Ledger and run an audit trail.

- Print invoices, credit notes and statements.

- Produce history and financial reports.

'Preparing to start' checklist

Before getting started, work through the checklist below.

- Check start date of your company's financial year.

- Check with accountant which VAT scheme is used.

Some things, such as the start date for the financial year, once entered cannot be changed, so do make sure you have all relevant information to hand before using Sage Instant Accounting for the first time.

- Draw up a list of defaults to use.

- Decide on a password if required.

- Backup the data if updating Sage.

- Have customer, supplier and bank details to hand.

- Product details.

- A list of all opening balances.

Starting Sage Instant Accounting

Altern- atively, if a shortcut has been set up on the Windows desktop, you can open Sage Instant Accounting by double-clicking on the icon.

Turn on your computer and when the Windows Desktop appears, do the following to start Instant Accounting 2000:

1 Click on Start.

2 Point to Programs – a selection appears.

3 Point to Sage.

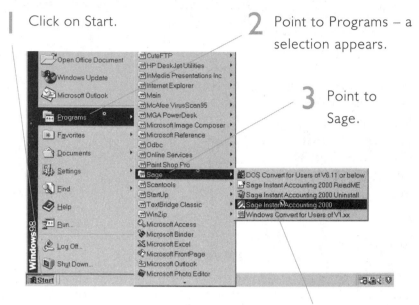

4 Click on Sage Instant Accounting.

When you run Instant Accounting 2000 for the first time, the Register Today dialog box appears and prompts you to register. You must register your product with Sage by following the on- screen instructions otherwise you will not be able to use the program for more than 30 uses or 30 days, whichever occurs first.

The Sage Instant Accounting desktop appears:

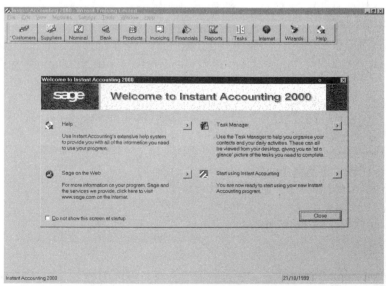

You can register your new program by telephone or via the Internet.

Settings

A quick method of accessing an option from the Menu bar is to hold down the Alt key and press the underlined letter of the function required (i.e., Alt+S pulls down the Settings menu).

Before Instant Accounting can be used there are a number of settings and defaults that need to be entered. The rest of this chapter shows how to do this. When required, select the appropriate settings option from the following list:

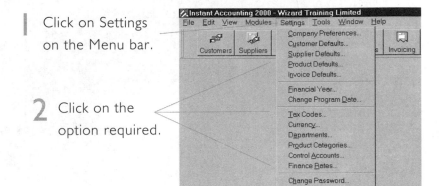

| Click on Settings on the Menu bar.

2 Click on the option required.

Click Help on the Sage Instant Accounting menu bar, then Shortcut Keys, to bring up a diagram of the available shortcuts. Click on the diagram to close it.

Using Passwords

The Data Protection Act requires that any system containing confidential information, i.e., financial details etc., should be protected against unauthorised access. Sage Instant Accounting uses a password to achieve this and once set, you will always be prompted for it at startup.

As with any password, you should never write it down if it can be avoided. Therefore, try to choose a password that is both easy for you to remember but difficult for someone else to discover. You can decrease the chance of somebody accidentally finding out your password by using a mixture of letters and numbers instead of an actual word.

Try to avoid using obvious things like a name, phone number or car registration as a password. These are too easy to guess.

| From the Settings menu click on Change Password.

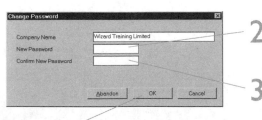

2 Type your password here.

3 Repeat the password here for confirmation.

4 Click OK to save password.

Company Preferences

Use the Tab key instead of your mouse to move onto the next line or box.

If you are unfamiliar with Sage Instant Accounting 2000, you may prefer to set up all of your details using the Easy Startup Wizard, which activates when Instant Accounting 2000 is run for the first time. You can also start this from the menu bar by selecting Modules, Wizards, then Easy Startup Wizard (see Page 27 for details).

You can assign your transactions to up to 999 different departments and divide Products into 999 different categories.

When you ran Instant Accounting for the first time the Easy Startup Wizard asked for your Company details. Alternatively, after selecting Company Preferences from the settings options, you can enter these details as follows:

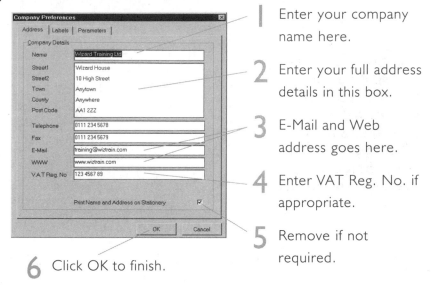

1 Enter your company name here.

2 Enter your full address details in this box.

3 E-Mail and Web address goes here.

4 Enter VAT Reg. No. if appropriate.

5 Remove if not required.

6 Click OK to finish.

Departments and Product Categories

For analysis purposes, you can assign transactions to different departments and divide products into different categories. To set up each of these:

1 Click on the required settings option and select the first blank entry.

2 Click Edit to bring up the Edit box.

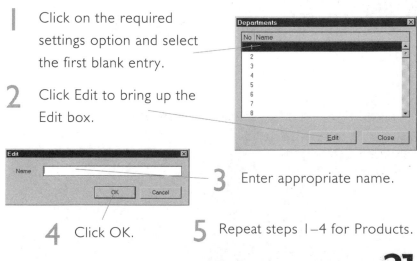

3 Enter appropriate name.

4 Click OK.

5 Repeat steps 1–4 for Products.

Setting up and checking Tax Codes

Instant Accounting already has the standard UK and EC VAT Rates set for you together with the code T1 (standard rate – currently 17.5%) set as the default tax code. Here is a list of the codes automatically set up during installation:

It is important to use the correct VAT codes. If unsure of current UK or EU VAT Tax rates then contact Customs and Excise.

T0	–	zero rated transactions
T1	–	standard rate
T2	–	exempt transactions
T4	–	sales to customers in EC*
T7	–	zero rated purchases from suppliers in EC*
T8	–	standard rated purchases from suppliers in EC*
T9	–	transactions not involving VAT

(* Outside the UK)

99 VAT codes are available in Instant Accounting. To enter or change VAT tax rates:

T1 is the standard rate code.

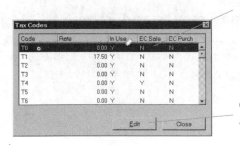

1 Choose Tax Codes after clicking on Settings on the menu bar, then select the required code.

2 Click Edit to bring up the Edit Tax Code box.

3 Enter percentage rate.

4 Click here if VAT rate is for an EC Code.

5 Select an EC Purchases and Sales link if appropriate.

6 Click OK, then Close the Tax Codes box.

...cont'd

Once transactions have been posted in your Sage Instant Accounting program, the Financial Year cannot be changed.

Financial Year

The start of the financial year is entered during the installation of Sage Instant Accounting or before entering any transactions:

1 From Settings on the menu bar Click on Financial Year then select the first month of your year from the list.

2 Enter the year if not correct.

3 Click OK.

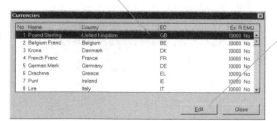

Currency

Initially Sage Instant Accounting 2000 is already set up with the currencies of the EC countries. These details can be edited or other countries set up as required:

1 Click on Currency and highlight the currency you want to edit or select the first available blank record to enter a new currency.

For further information about the Euro currency and the Economic Monetary Union (EMU), visit the Sage website at www.sage.com, where you will find links to other related information sources.

2 Click Edit to bring up the Edit Currency box.

3 Enter the name of the Currency.

4 Enter the Country here.

5 The EC Member code goes here.

6 Click OK, then Close.

Customer and Supplier Defaults

When creating a new customer or supplier, details about credit limit, terms, discount etc. are needed. Customer and Supplier records are fully discussed in Chapters Three and Four respectively but before this, however, defaults need setting up.

 For customers, default nominal codes (N/C) start at 4000.

1 Select Customer Defaults from the Settings options.

2 Select this Tab to enter the defaults for your customer records.

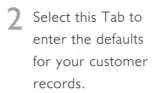

 Remember that all of your Customer and Supplier defaults can also be entered in one go through the Easy Startup wizard.

3 Click on the relevant Tabs to enter Statements and Ageing Balance defaults.

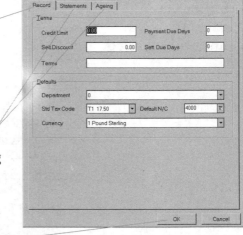

4 Click OK to save Customer Defaults.

5 Select Supplier Defaults from the Settings options.

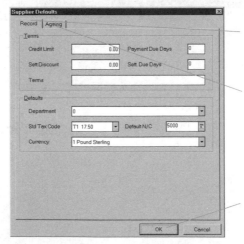

6 Enter relevant Supplier Defaults here.

 Default nominal codes for suppliers start at 5000.

7 Select this Tab to enter Aged Balances Period, specifying calendar months or days.

8 Click OK to save Supplier Defaults.

Product Defaults

Defaults also need to be set up for Products:

1 Select Product Defaults from the Settings options.

 You can use the Finder button on the right of the Nominal Code box to speed up entry.

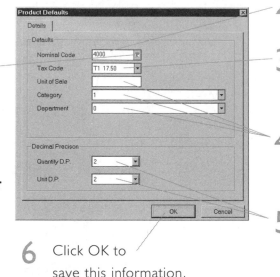

2 Enter the Nominal account code here.

3 Allocate the correct Tax Code for the Product.

 The Finder button is also a quick way of creating a new Nominal Code.

4 Complete the rest of the defaults as necessary.

5 Enter the Decimal Point placing for the product.

6 Click OK to save this information.

Control Accounts

Sage Instant Accounting uses Control Accounts to make automatic double-entry postings to the ledger.

1 To view or edit these Nominal Codes select Control Accounts from the Settings options.

 Unless you have created your own Chart of Accounts, the Control accounts should never need changing.

2 To change a Control account click on the nominal code and type the new code or use the Finder button.

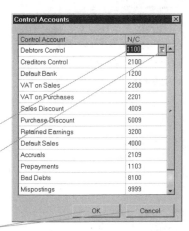

3 Click OK to save and close or Cancel to abandon changes.

Finance Rates

Finance rates need to be set up before any credit charges can be applied to your customers.

When a Finance Charge Rate is applied to a transaction, the first rate charged will be applied monthly until the invoice is paid.

1 Click on the Finance Rates option from the Settings menu to bring up the Finance Charge Rates box.

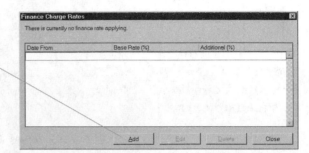

2 Click on Add to enter a new finance rate charge.

3 Enter the date the charge is to be applied from.

Use the Delete button on the Finance Charge Rates window to remove any unwanted charges.

4 Enter the Base Rate as a percentage here.

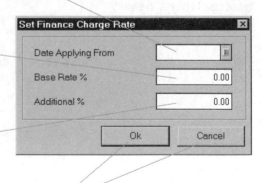

5 Enter an additional charge here if applicable.

6 Click OK to save new finance rate or Cancel to return to the Finance Charge Rates box.

7 Click Close to finish.

Easy Startup Wizard

 To run the Easy Startup Wizard simply open the File menu and choose **Run Easy Startup wizard.**

If you are new to Sage Instant Accounting, the Easy Startup Wizard will guide you through the process of entering the default settings needed before you can start using it. The following screen shows the Key areas you can select for your business as you work through the process:

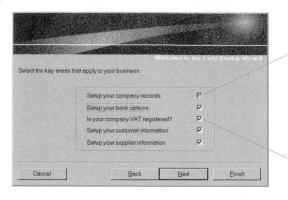

 You can also activate the Easy Startup Wizard by clicking on Modules in the menu bar, then Wizards and Easy Startup Wizard.

| If you have already entered some information, it will be indicated like this.

2 Tick only if VAT registered.

 You can exit the Easy Startup Wizard at any time. You may, for example, need some information before you can complete a particular section. Simply choose to exit the Wizard and select to carry on from that point the next time you run it again.

Before running the Easy Startup Wizard, you will need to have available the following information ready to enter:

Company Records	Name, Address, Postcode
	Web Site and E-mail address
	Telephone and Fax numbers
	Financial Year start date
Banking Information	All Bank Account details
VAT Information	VAT Registration Number
	VAT Registration Scheme
Customer and Supplier Information	Ageing Periods
	Credit Limit
	Standard Terms
	Payment Due Days
	Nominal Code and VAT Rate

The Sage Instant Accounting 2000 Toolbar

 If any of the Toolbar options do not appear onscreen, click on the arrow button on the left or right of the Toolbar to display them.

From the toolbar the user selects an accounting option by clicking on the relevant button. Alternatively, the required function can be selected from the Modules option on the Menu bar.

 Opens the Customer (sales) Ledger.

 Opens the Supplier (purchase) Ledger.

 Opens the Nominal Ledger.

 To access the Bank, Credit Cards and Petty Cash accounts.

 Opens the Product Records and Stock accounts.

 To generate Invoices, Credits and related reports.

 To access Financial functions (i.e., Profit and Loss, Audit Trail, Trial Balance, VAT).

 Opens the Report Designer window.

 Opens the Instant Accounting Task Manager window.

 Runs the Internet Browser.

 Brings up a menu of Wizards options.

Brings up a menu of Help options.

 To make the buttons more distinct, select Tools then Options from the menu bar, then check the Show Button Frames box.

 For quick access to the Sage Web site, just click on the Internet button.

The Customer Ledger

In this chapter you will learn how to use the Customer (Sales) Ledger to maintain customer records and create new ones as well as entering credit notes and invoices. You will also be shown how to view transaction activity as well as produce an overdue payments letter, and will learn how to apply credit charges and place an account on hold.

Covers

Chapter Three

The Importance of Keeping a Financial System

It is essential for all businesses to have a system to record and monitor their business and financial transactions. This information needs to be accurately recorded and kept as up to date as possible if it is to present a true financial position.

Such a system will involve the recording of transactions using the traditional method of bookkeeping or advanced accounting procedures, where financial reports (i.e., profit and loss statements and balance sheet, etc.) can be produced.

These reports provide Management with information on sales, purchases, turnover, expenses, debtors and creditors, assets and liabilities, and more important, if the business has made a profit.

The Inland Revenue and HM Customs and Excise (if VAT registered) will also need accurate accounts, which must conform to general bookkeeping and accounting procedures.

This information is also of importance to your Bank Manager, especially if there is a need to borrow money to ease cash flow problems or help set up a new business venture. Likewise, potential investors in your business may first want to see the true financial position of your accounts before making a decision.

Computerised systems have now removed the majority of time consuming and repetitive tasks of manual accounting. Businesses can check their financial status on a daily basis, or over a designated period of time. This valuable information will aid important decision making and business planning and is crucial for forecasting whether a business will succeed or fail.

The Customers Toolbar

The Customers toolbar provides features for creating customer records, viewing the activity of customer transactions, producing invoices and credit notes, viewing aged balances and applying credit charges. Customer Statements are produced here as well as letters and a wide range of reports.

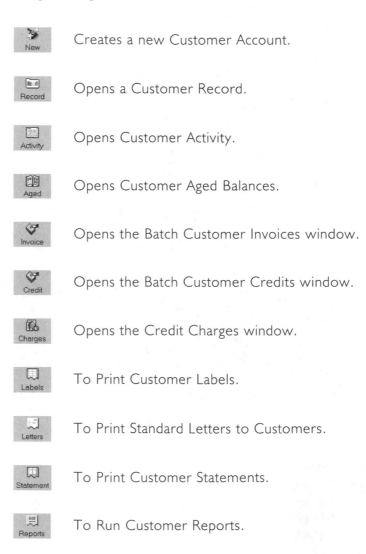

Creates a new Customer Account.

Opens a Customer Record.

Opens Customer Activity.

Opens Customer Aged Balances.

Opens the Batch Customer Invoices window.

Opens the Batch Customer Credits window.

Opens the Credit Charges window.

To Print Customer Labels.

To Print Standard Letters to Customers.

To Print Customer Statements.

To Run Customer Reports.

Creating Customer Records

 Use the New wizard for simple step by step instructions for entering a new customer record.

 Always start by entering the Account Code first. Each customer is given a unique A/C code of up to 8 characters. Use the finder button to locate existing codes.

 Before you enter an Opening Balance you must have first saved the new customer details.

 The method of entering opening balances is different for Standard VAT and VAT Cash Accounting. Use F1 help key to check.

Within this window, a customer record can be added, edited or deleted. You can also record agreed credit terms and even check how sales are progressing compared to a similar period the year before.

1 Select Customers from the Sage Instant Accounting toolbar, then click on Record to bring up the Customer Record window.

2 Use Details to store customer name, address and contact information.

3 Use the O/B button to enter an Opening Balance where required.

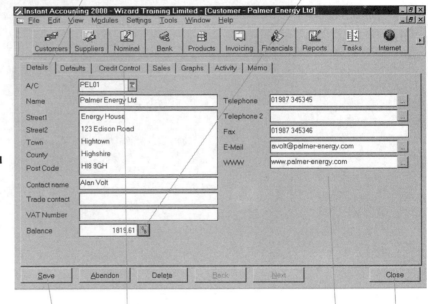

4 Use the Credit Control tab to enter credit terms agreed with the customer.

5 Enter contact information here.

6 Click Save to store the Customer Record.

7 Enter a new record or click Close to finish.

...cont'd

 Use Activity to quickly view a customer's outstanding balance, Aged Debts etc.

 These codes identify the transaction type:

SI = Sales Invoice.

SR = Sales Receipt.

SC = Sales Credit Note.

SD = Discount.

SA = Sales Receipt on Account.

 Use the Tidy button to clear all transaction sub-items from view.

 To view this screen from the Customers window, select the customer required and then click on the Activity button.

Viewing transactions

Once customer activity has taken place, Sage Instant Accounting offers you a variety of options for checking customer transaction details:

- View customer invoices, receipts, credit notes and balances on a monthly basis, as a graph or table.

- Use the Activity option to see a breakdown of each customer's transactions.

- View or print the Customer's aged balances.

1 Click on the Activity tab in the Customer Record window.

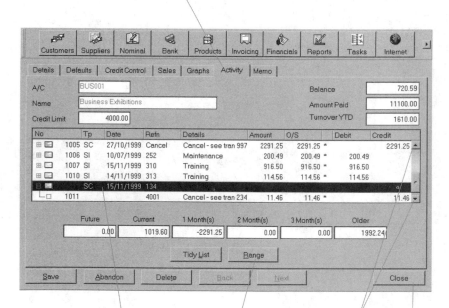

2 Double click on a transaction to show all items.

3 Click on the arrows to scroll through all the transactions.

4 Click on Range to select another date range or range of transactions, then click OK.

5 Select Close to return to Customer window.

Batch Customer Invoice

Invoices are important business transaction documents and record detailed information about the goods or services supplied to the customer. Briefly, these details include the invoice number, name and address of customer, date of sale, details of goods and or services supplied, details of discount, total amount of money due and terms of trade.

If you know the first character of the customer A/C, enter it and choose the Finder button to automatically bring up the first code beginning with this character.

There are different types of invoices for the task you are carrying out and Chapter Eight explains this in detail and shows you how to create a product or a service invoice. However, any invoices produced manually (Batch Invoices) and sent to customers need recording. No printout is produced.

To record a batch customer invoice do the following:

1 Choose Invoice from the Customers toolbar.

2 Enter the customer Account Code or use the finder button to display a list of codes.

3 Change invoice date if different from current system date.

Where you only know the gross value of an invoice, enter it in the Net box and use the Calculate Net button to work out the correct Net value and VAT due.

4 Enter the Invoice Number here and a Reference Number, if required.

A/C	Date	Inv No.	Refn	N/C	Dept	Details	Net	T/C	VAT
FEL01	25/10/1999			4000	0		0.00	T1	0.00

A/C Name: Palmer Energy Ltd
N/C Name: Sales Type A
Tax Rate: 17.50
Batch Total: 0.00

Save   Abandon   Calculate Net   Close

5 Change Nominal Code or Department if different from defaults.

Always check that the correct Tax Code is used. See Page 22.

7 Click Save to update the nominal ledger and customer details (details posted), then Close.

6 Enter Net value of invoice here.

Batch Customer Credit Note

A credit note is used, for example, where an error is made and a customer has been overcharged on an invoice, Sometimes, damaged goods are returned and so a credit note is issued showing the amount due to the customer.

Like batch invoicing, credit notes processed manually need entering. To record batch credit notes:

To check the credit note has been posted, make a note of the balance for the appropriate customer in the Customers window before entering the credit note, then check that the balance has reduced by the correct amount after performing Step 6.

1 Click Credit from the Customers toolbar to bring up the Batch Customer Credits window.

2 Enter the customer Account Code.

3 The screen displays the defaults for the nominal account code posting, VAT rate to be applied and department.

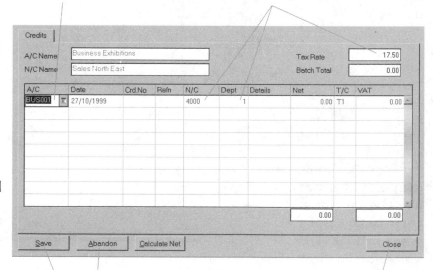

If you need a printout of a credit, generate a product or service credit note from Invoicing on the Sage Instant Accounting toolbar and the details will be recorded automatically.

4 Enter credit details for each customer in the same way as for batch invoice.

5 Check all values are correct and click Save to post the details or Abandon to start again.

6 Click Close to return to the Customers window.

Customer Aged Balance

To identify debtors and monitor cashflow, customers' outstanding balances and transactions need to be regularly checked. These transactions are grouped by the age of the debt, either on calendar months or based on a period of days, e.g. 30, 60 and 90 days etc. Debt chasing letters can be issued if required. Some businesses may use this information to calculate interest charges for late payment.

Use Customer Defaults from the Settings menu, then select the Ageing tab to change the age of the debt between calendar months and period of days.

1 From the Customers window select the required customer.

2 Click Aged to bring up the Aged Balances Date Defaults box.

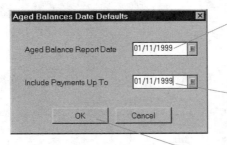

3 Enter the date to be used for calculating the aged balances.

4 To include payments only up to a particular date, enter that date here.

When viewing aged balances in graphical format use the Options facility to select what information you wish to view in the graph.

6 To see the aged balances in graphical format use the Graph tab.

5 Click OK to bring up the Aged Balances window.

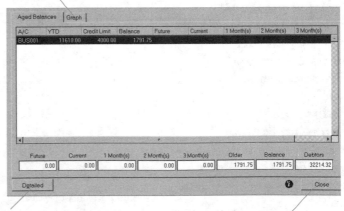

7 For a transaction breakdown click on Detailed.

8 Click Close to return.

Credit Charges

Interest rates applied to credit charges are set using the Finance Rates option from the Settings menu.

Use the Memo box to keep notes on a credit agreement negotiated with the selected customer.

Since November 1998, credit charges can be applied for customers whose payments are overdue. To apply this, from the Customers window click Charges to run the Credit Charges Wizard, then follow the instructions.

Before you can use the Wizard, finance rates must have first been set up.

A payment which is 30 days overdue is regarded, by default, as late. If you need to change payment terms, do the following:

1 From the Instant Accounting toolbar choose the Customers button.

2 Highlight the appropriate customer or customers, then click the Record button.

3 Click on the Credit Control tab to bring up the Credit Control details box.

4 Enter new details in Pay Due Days.

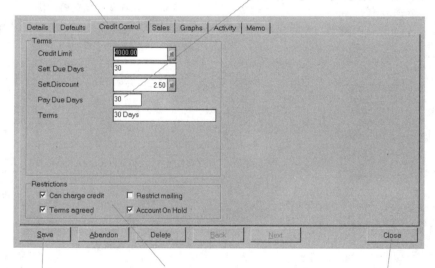

5 Apply account restrictions here if desired, such as placing account on hold, allowing credit to be charged etc.

6 Change any of the other terms as required, then click Save.

7 Click Close to return to the Customers window, then Close again.

Applying Credit Charges

The introduction in November 1998 of 'The Late Payments Of Commercial Debts (Interest) Act 1998' has given small firms the statutory right to charge interest from larger businesses on overdue invoices. The right to claim interest is not compulsory and the decision of whether or not to do so rests with the individual business.

If you need to check on the base rate for a particular period simply call the Bank of England (currently 0171 601 4878). It can provide the current base rate as well as past base rates.

The new legislation classes a payment as late if it does not arrive within the agreed terms or, if no payment period has been set, within 30 days. If, for example, the payment terms are set at 30 days and payment is not received within this period, then interest can be charged from day 31.

The rate of interest that you can charge is the Bank of England base rate plus 8%. The base rate used to calculate the interest due is the rate in force at the end of the day on which the contract is to be made. The interest rate applied is set in the Finance Rates option from the Settings menu. Only one finance rate can be applied to an invoice.

To be able to apply late payment terms you must enter a value in the 'Pay Due Days' text box in the Customer Record, Credit Control Tab (See Page 37, Step 4), then tick the 'Can charge credit' check box (Step 5). Then use the Credit Charges Wizard to guide you through the process of applying credit charges to overdue outstanding transactions.

Whilst the Act allows small firms to claim interest from large businesses it does not allow large businesses to claim interest from small businesses.

To set up a Finance Rate:

1 From the Settings menu click Finance Rates, then click Add.

2 Enter the Finance Rate details here.

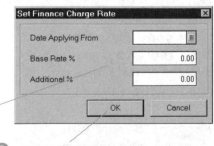

3 Click OK, then Close.

To run the Credit Charges Wizard, from the Customers window toolbar click on the Charges option and follow the instructions.

Customer Letters and Labels

Occasionally you may have a need to send standard information to a customer, such as change of address, or to chase up an overdue payment. All of the necessary information needed for these letters is taken from your records.

A number of the more common standard letters are provided with Sage Instant Accounting, but alternatively there is also the option to create new ones. The new letters can be stored for future use.

1 From the Customers window, select the customer or customers you want to send a letter to.

2 Click the Letters button on the Customers toolbar to bring up the Customer Letters list.

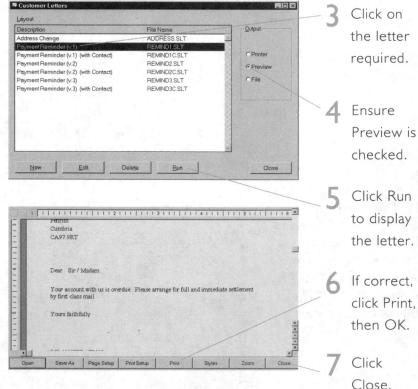

3 Click on the letter required.

4 Ensure Preview is checked.

5 Click Run to display the letter.

6 If correct, click Print, then OK.

7 Click Close.

Labels

To help speed up the process of sending correspondence to customers use the standard layout label files to print out their names and addresses on predefined labels, or alternatively, create your own.

You have the option as to what data is printed on the label and how the labels are positioned on a page.

Use the Zoom button if you need to decrease or increase the amount of the page on view. This option lets you zoom in on labels so you can check if they are correct, or to view them as laid out on the page. Note that whilst this is not the same as changing the size of the document window it does have a similar effect.

1 From the Customers window, select the customer or customers you want to print labels for.

2 Click the Labels button on the Customers toolbar to bring up the Customer Labels list.

3 Click on the label type required.

4 Ensure Preview is checked.

To produce labels for all your customers in one go, make sure no customers are selected in Step 1 by pressing the Clear button, then carry out Steps 2–7.

5 Click Run to produce and display the labels.

6 If correct click Print, then OK.

7 Click Close, then close each window.

The Customer Statement

To keep customers up to date about their financial position customer statements should be sent out on a regular basis, normally once a month. The statement shows details of all recorded customer transactions, together with a balance figure.

You can also use the Customer Statement window to delete statements no longer required, or to modify and design your own statements.

I From the Customers window click on the Statements button to bring up the Customer Statements window.

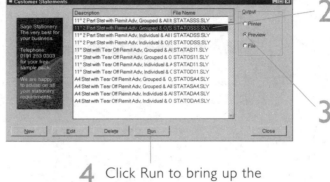

2 Choose the statement layout you require.

3 Ensure Preview is checked.

4 Click Run to bring up the Criteria box.

If you need a copy of the statement saving on disk use the Save As button in the statement preview window and give the statement a file name. You can then open and print the statement at a later date, if required.

5 Enter Customer Reference range.

6 Enter Transaction Date from and to.

7 Click OK to preview statement.

8 Use the Zoom button on the preview to zoom in or out if you need to check any statement details.

9 When satisfied, click Print to print the statement, then Close all windows.

Customer Reports

The arrows on the Customers toolbar let you scroll across all available buttons.

Sage Instant Accounting provides you with a wide range of ready designed customer reports to suit the majority of needs. To print or view a customer report, do the following:

1 Click on the Reports button in the Customers window.

2 Select the report you require from the Supplier Reports list.

Also use this report window to create, edit or delete Customer Reports.

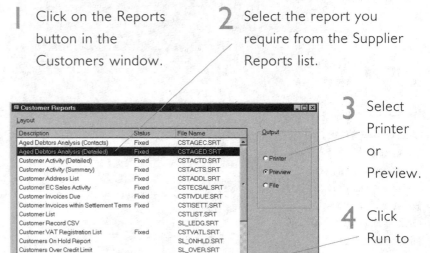

3 Select Printer or Preview.

4 Click Run to generate the report.

An additional Criteria box may appear for some reports for you to enter ranges, such as Customer Reference etc.

If a Criteria box appears when you run the report, you will need to enter appropriate information as follows:

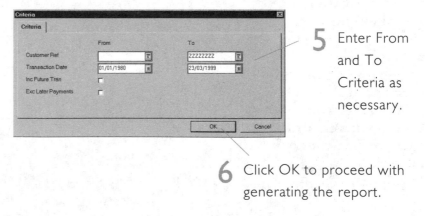

Use the Reports feature regularly to print out useful information about your customers, such as Aged Debtors, Invoices Due etc.

5 Enter From and To Criteria as necessary.

6 Click OK to proceed with generating the report.

7 If correct, print the report, then Close all windows.

The Supplier Ledger

This chapter shows you how to create and maintain supplier records within the Suppliers (Purchase) Ledger. Through recording invoices and credit notes you receive you can see how much you owe and when these payments are due. You will learn how to view details of any invoices received and payments made to suppliers using tables, graphs and reports as well as how to generate standard letters and mailing labels for all or selected suppliers.

Covers

Chapter Four

The Supplier Toolbar

The Supplier toolbar has many similar buttons to the Customer toolbar, and again provides you with facilities for setting up records, checking supplier activity, recording invoices, credit notes, mailing functions and reporting.

Creates a new Supplier Record.

Opens a Supplier Record.

View Supplier Activity.

View Supplier Aged Balances.

Record Supplier Invoices.

Record Supplier Credit Notes.

To Print Supplier Labels.

To Print Standard Letters to Suppliers.

To Run Customer Reports.

Creating Supplier Records

Within this window you can view, edit or delete a supplier record. A new supplier record can also be added if you have all of the details to hand. To add a new supplier first select Suppliers from the Sage Instant Accounting toolbar, then do the following:

 Until you are familiar with Sage Instant Accounting 2000, use the New wizard for simple step by step instructions for entering a new supplier record.

1 Click on Record to bring up the Supplier Record window.

2 Use Details to enter supplier information, such as name, address and contact details.

3 Use the O/B button to enter an Opening Balance where required.

 Always start with the A/C when entering a new record.

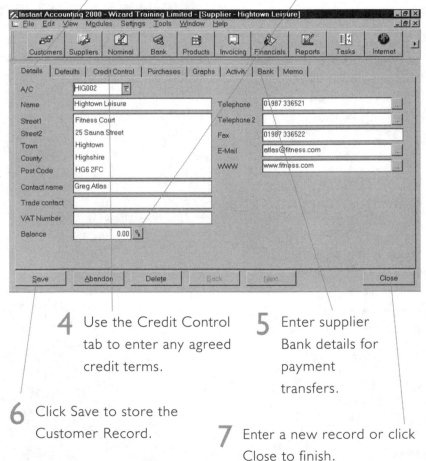

To help save time later, enter accurately as much detail into the record as possible.

4 Use the Credit Control tab to enter any agreed credit terms.

5 Enter supplier Bank details for payment transfers.

6 Click Save to store the Customer Record.

7 Enter a new record or click Close to finish.

Using Criteria

This useful Criteria feature is also available within other program windows, such as Customers, Products, Nominal and Invoicing etc.

Use Criteria from the Customers window as a quick means of looking something up about your customers, such as a list of those who have exceeded their credit limit, or whose accounts are on hold. You can even use Criteria to search for a supplier or customer if, say, you only have a single item of detail to hand, such as a telephone number or department, provided this information has been entered when setting up the record.

The Criteria function available within the suppliers window can help save you valuable time when searching for specific information regarding supplier transactions. The following example shows you how to produce a list of suppliers you owe money to:

1 Click the Criteria button in the bottom left hand corner of the Suppliers window to bring up the Criteria window.

2 Click on the Amounts tab.

3 Tick the Balance check box.

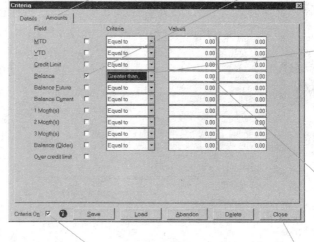

4 Select 'Greater than' from the Criteria drop down list.

5 Enter 0 (zero) here.

6 Tick the Criteria On check box.

7 Click Close to return to the Suppliers window.

8 Note that the Criteria button is now highlighted and the only records displayed are those that match the given criteria.

9 To cancel the criteria function repeat Steps 6 and 7, this time removing the tick.

Supplier Activity

To view this screen from the Supplier Record window, enter the A/C for the supplier required (if none selected) and then click on the Activity tab.

This feature enables you to view each supplier's transactions in detail. If less complete information is required, you can define a transaction or date range to limit the view:

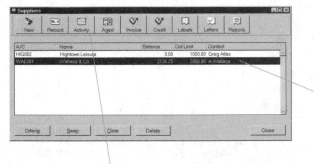

| From the Suppliers window, click on the supplier you want to look at.

Use the Tidy button to clear all transaction sub-items from view.

2 Click on Activity.

3 In the next box enter the transaction and/or date ranges.

4 Click OK to bring up the Activity window.

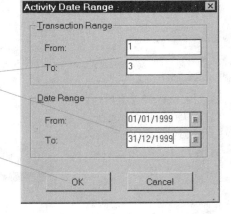

These codes identify the transaction type:

PI = Purchase Invoice.

PP = Purchase Payment.

PC = Purchase Credit Note.

PD = Discount on a Purchase Payment.

PA = Purchase Payment on Account.

5 Double-click a transaction for more details.

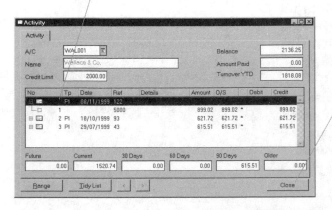

6 Click Close to return to the Suppliers window.

Supplier Aged Balance

The age period is set through Supplier Defaults from the Settings menu. You can base it on either calendar months or a period of days, specified by you. Remember also that ageing is relative to the program date.

Aged balance is the term given to the time lapse of outstanding debt, whether owed to or by you. Sage Instant Accounting lets you view the amount of money you owe your Suppliers, grouped on the age of the debt. It is common practice for businesses to give 30 days credit, but others terms are sometimes negotiated. Sage Instant Accounting default aged periods are 30, 60 and 90 days.

1 From the Suppliers window, click on the supplier you require and select the Aged button from the toolbar.

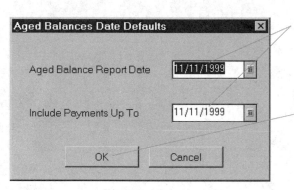

2 Enter appropriate dates here.

3 Click OK to display the Aged Balances Report.

If you need to enter a date only a few days either side of that displayed simply use the cursor up or down keys on the keyboard.

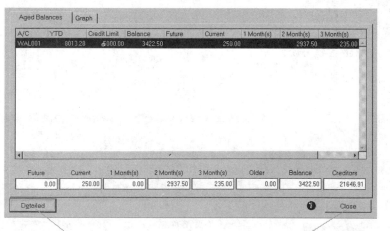

From November 1998 legislation took effect that enables small businesses (less than 50 employees) to charge interest on late payments from large businesses.

4 To see the transactions which make up the aged balance click Detailed.

5 Close each window when finished.

Recording Supplier Invoices

Invoices received from your suppliers can be entered a few at a time using the Batch Supplier Invoices window. You have full flexibility using this option, such as posting each invoice item to a different nominal account if need be, or allocating to a different VAT code, such as from default VAT to zero VAT. To enter invoices, do the following:

Always check the correct tax code has been selected for the VAT to avoid errors later. Instant Accounting enters T1 (standard rate) for you by default. You may need to change this to T0 for transactions which are zero rated or to T9 for those not involving VAT.

1 From the Suppliers window click Invoice to bring up the Batch Supplier Invoices window.

2 Type the supplier's account code here or use the Finder button.

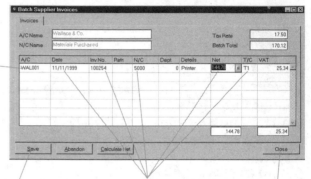

3 Enter the Date and other invoice details, then check the Nominal (N/C) and Tax (T/C) codes and amend if necessary.

'Posting' means updating the Nominal ledger and relevant supplier's details. If you do not wish to save this batch, choose the Abandon button to clear the data and start again.

4 When all details are correct and all invoices have been entered, click Save to post the details.

5 Click Close to return to the Suppliers window.

6 Note that the Supplier's record now displays the new balance, then click Close again.

Recording Supplier Credit Notes

Occasionally goods ordered from suppliers may arrive damaged or incomplete. The supplier issues you a credit note reducing the amount owed. Credit notes are recorded using the Credit option from the Suppliers window.

 To see if there is more detail to an entry, just double-click on that entry line.

If a credit note contains a number of items, for your benefit it is advisable to enter each transaction individually, but giving them the same account code, date and reference. Sage Instant Accounting will group these together and list them as a single credit note. You can then view the note in detail using Activity from the Suppliers window.

 It is always advisable to check the changes you have made by noting the before and after outstanding balance. This will save time later should a mistake have been made.

1 To record a credit note, from the Suppliers window click Credit.

2 Enter the supplier Account Code. Use the Finder button if you don't have the code.

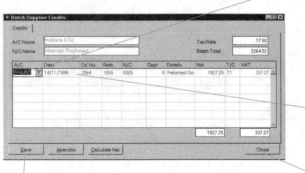

3 Enter the credit note date.

4 Enter the remaining details and check that they are correct.

6 Click Close to return to the Suppliers window.

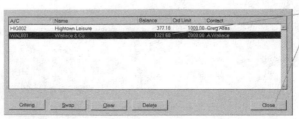

5 Click Save to update the nominal ledger and record the credit details.

7 Note that the outstanding balance has changed and click Close.

 It is useful to enter the invoice number that the credit note refers to in the Reference (Refn) box for identification. This will appear in the details under Financials.

Supplier Mailing Letters and Labels

As with Customers, Sage Instant Accounting includes the facility to produce preformatted letters and labels for your suppliers. You can create whatever standard letters or label layouts you wish. All the necessary address information etc. is taken from the stored supplier details.

To produce letters or labels for certain suppliers only, click on those suppliers to select them in the Suppliers window before performing Steps 1–5. If, however, you want to print letters or labels for all your suppliers, ensure none are selected by clicking on the Clear button in the Suppliers window.

To produce the standard letter informing suppliers of your change of address, do the following:

1 From the Suppliers window click Letters to bring up the Supplier Letters window.

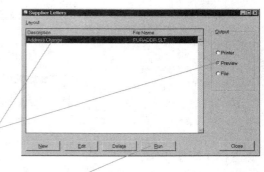

2 Click on the letter required and ensure Preview is checked.

3 Click Run.

4 Check the letters and click Print, then OK in the Printer box.

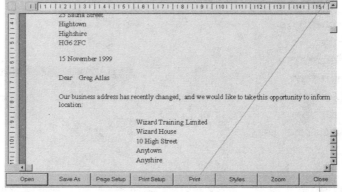

Always remember to check that the correct paper, labels and printer type have been selected before printing if you want to avoid wasting time and paper.

5 When finished, Close all windows.

Labels

To produce address labels for your suppliers, select the Labels button from the Supplier window then carry out Steps 2–5 as above.

Supplier Reports

Sage Instant Accounting sets up a number of reports ready to use at installation, to suit most requirements.

You can generate a wide range of detailed reports about your suppliers. These reports are produced from the information you entered about suppliers and their transactions. Whilst Sage Instant Accounting already has a considerable number of reports set up, if any further reports are required you can create them using the Report Designer. To run or view a supplier report:

1 Click on the Reports button in the Suppliers window.

2 Select the report you require from the Supplier Reports list.

A Criteria box will appear when you click Run on most reports for you to enter ranges, such as Supplier Reference, Transaction Date etc.

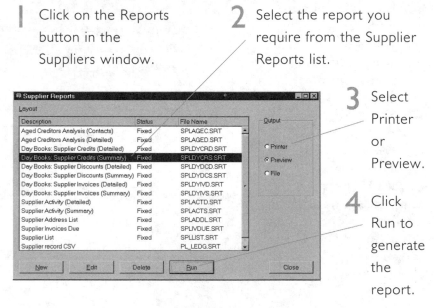

3 Select Printer or Preview.

4 Click Run to generate the report.

From the Suppliers Reports window you can also edit or delete an existing report or create a new one.

5 If a Criteria box appears, enter the From and To details, then click OK.

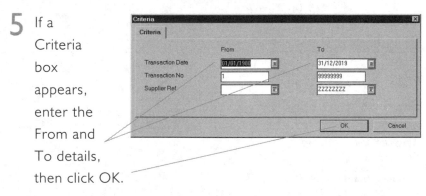

To learn how to create a new report, or edit an existing one, refer to Chapter 10.

6 After printing, Close all windows.

The Nominal Ledger

This chapter explains the important role played by the Nominal Ledger and how its accounts detail the flow of money in and out of the business. You will be shown how to analyse these account transactions using tables, graphs and transaction activity reports so you can control and monitor finances through making informed business decisions. You can even tailor your own Nominal Ledger set of accounts to meet specific business needs.

Covers

Chapter Five

The Nominal Toolbar

The Nominal toolbar buttons provide you with facilities for setting up records, viewing account activity, making journal entries, working on the chart of accounts and reporting.

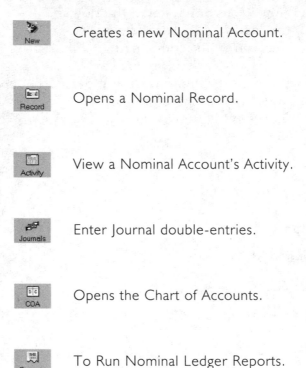

Creates a new Nominal Account.

Opens a Nominal Record.

View a Nominal Account's Activity.

Enter Journal double-entries.

Opens the Chart of Accounts.

To Run Nominal Ledger Reports.

The Nominal Ledger

To create a new nominal account, click the New button from the Nominal window.

Click on a record to select or to deselect it. Use the Clear button to deselect all selected records.

Standard nominal accounts for Instant Accounting are:

- Asset Accounts from 0001 to 1999
- Liability Accounts from 2000 to 3999
- Income Accounts from 4000 to 4999
- Purchase Accounts from 5000 to 5999
- Direct Expenses from 6000 to 6999
- Overheads from 7000 to 9999.

The Nominal Ledger, also referred to as the General Ledger, is a grouped analysis of your sales and purchase transactions. For example, when a sales or purchase invoice is posted to the sales or purchase ledger, Sage Instant Accounting records it in the Nominal Ledger against the appropriate Nominal account number.

It therefore contains all the accounts for your business, e.g., sales, purchases, expenses, VAT, cash and bank, sundry income, fixed assets, liabilities, capital and owner's drawings, etc. However, it does not keep details of debtors and creditors. These are held in the respective sales and purchase ledgers.

The Nominal accounts let you see quickly where your money is. Information from here is used in the production of management reports to tell you how your business is performing.

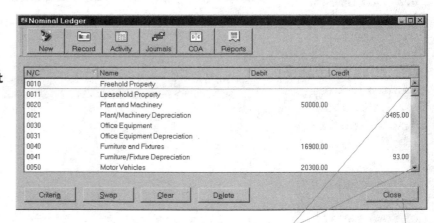

1 Click Nominal from the Instant Accounting toolbar to view the Nominal Ledger.

2 Use scroll bar to view range of accounts.

3 Click Close when done.

At installation, Sage Instant Accounting created a standard set of nominal accounts unless, in the Startup Wizard, you chose to create your own nominal structure. Note that the latter option only creates the Control Accounts for you.

Nominal Records

Check your business performance by initially entering monthly budget and prior year values, then regularly comparing these against the actual value.

You can tailor the nominal accounts to exactly meet your needs by using the Nominal Record window. You have the facility to add, edit and delete nominal accounts as well as viewing transactions posted to each account on a monthly basis.

Using the Record window you can also set budget values for each month of your financial year for a particular nominal account. You can also compare the actual monthly figures against the budget values to keep track of how close you are to meeting targets. To add a nominal account record do the following:

You can edit a Nominal Account to suit your needs. Simply use the Finder button for Step 2 to locate the N/C, then type any changes in the Details box and click on the Save button.

1 Click Record from the Nominal Ledger to bring up the Nominal Record window.

2 In the Details tab box, enter the new nominal account code here.

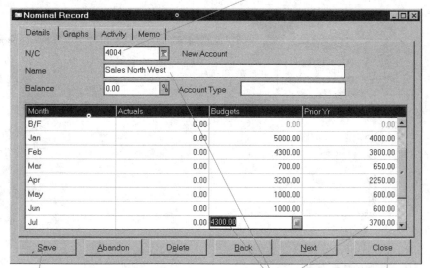

The New account details must first be saved before an Opening Balance can be entered.

3 Press the Tab key and note that this is a New Account.

4 Enter new account Name, Budget and Prior Year values.

5 Click Save to store details or Abandon to start again.

6 Click Close to return to the Nominal Ledger.

Viewing Nominal Transactions

You can view your Nominal Ledger transactions by using:

- Graphs.

- Activity reports.

- Table formats.

Transaction Analysis using Graphs

A range of 2D and 3D charts is available in Instant Accounting to visually compare your current year's trading against the previous year and any budgets you put in place.

You can save the graph to disk as a chart file. Click on the Disk icon and enter a file name.

Use this button to switch between 2D and 3D graph.

You can change what you view on the graph by clicking on the Options button and altering the View or Compare selection.

1 From the Nominal Ledger window, select the nominal account you wish to view.

2 Click Record, then select the Graphs tab to display data in graphical form.

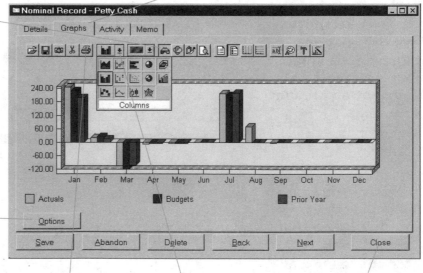

3 To choose a different type of graph, click here, then click on the graph required.

4 Click on the Printer button to print out the graph.

5 Click Close to return to the Nominal Ledger window.

...cont'd

Viewing Nominal Account Activity

You will occasionally need to view transactions that have been posted to the nominal ledger accounts. To do this from the Nominal Ledger window:

Transactions already cleared from the audit trail are shown as a single carried forward total and displayed as an Opening Balance (O/BAL).

1 Click on the nominal account you wish to view.

2 Click on the Activity button to bring up the Defaults box.

3 Enter the appropriate Transaction and Date ranges.

4 Click OK to display Activity.

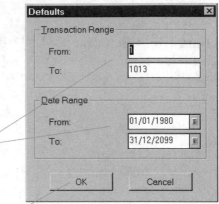

Each line of the Activity list box represents a single invoice, credit note, payment on account or receipt.

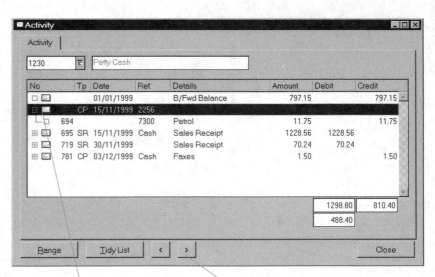

You can select more than one account to view at a time and simply use the '<' and '>' arrow buttons to scroll through them.

5 Double-click a transaction to view any further details.

7 Click Close to return to the Nominal Ledger.

6 Use the arrow buttons to view other nominal accounts, if more than one was selected in Step 1.

The Ref. column in the Activity window shows the reference given to the transaction when it was posted.

Transaction Codes

Transactions in the Activity window are identified by a type (Tp) or transaction code, allocated by Instant Accounting. The following is a list of transaction codes used:

BR (Bank Receipt)	SD (Discount on Sales Receipt)
BP (Bank Payment)	SA (Sales Receipt on Account)
CP (Cash Payment)	PI (Purchase Invoice)
CR (Cash Receipt)	PP (Purchase Payment)
JD (Journal Debit)	PC (Purchase Credit Note)
JC (Journal Credit)	PD (Discount on Purchase Payment)
SI (Sales Invoice)	PA (Purchase Payment on Account)
SR (Sales Receipt)	VP (Credit Payments)
SC (Sales Credit)	VR (Credit Receipts)

You can tell at a glance if criteria is being applied to a list because the text on the Criteria button will be bold.

Using Criteria

It is sometimes handy to reduce the number of records displayed in the Nominal Ledger window or on your reports to only those that match a specific criteria. This will save you having to search through too many records just to find the information you need. For example, this is how to list only control accounts in the Nominal Ledger window:

1 Click Criteria in the Nominal Ledger window.

2 Tick Account type.

Criteria remains applied to a list until the tick entered in Step 4 is removed. Performing Steps 1, 4 and 5 will do this for you.

3 Select Equal to and Control Account here.

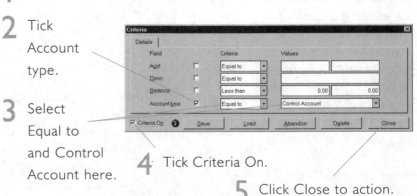

4 Tick Criteria On.

5 Click Close to action.

The Journal

The rules for debits and credits are: Debit the account which receives the value. Credit the account which gives the value.

The Journal allows you to make transfers between any of your nominal account codes regardless of type (Asset, Liability, Income or Expenditure), provided you adhere to double-entry bookkeeping principles. It lets you enter transactions which may not be covered within the standard Sage Instant Accounting facilities.

It is a useful source of reference for these non-regular transactions and can reduce errors by providing a list (audit trail) for checking purposes. Examples of these transactions include correction of errors, transfer of monies, as well as the purchase and sale of fixed assets on credit.

Double-Entry Bookkeeping

Do not be confused by the double-entry system when it comes to bank transfers. Your bank is a separate entity to your business and you are their customer. Consequently, in the ledger, your bank account balances are shown in the Debit column, so when you make a double entry transfer you will debit the account receiving the money and Credit the account the money is being transferred from. See the example on Page 61.

Unless you are familiar with accounting principles, double-entry bookkeeping could appear confusing, so here is a simple explanation. As the term 'bookkeeping' implies, your transactions are recorded in a kind of a book. Double-entry bookkeeping simply means that there will be two entries for each transaction in that book.

The 'ledger' is the term given to the main book in which you make your entries. A double-entry format ledger has two sides to it, the left always being referred to as the Debit side and the right the Credit side.

With Sage Instant Accounting, instead of a real book, you use a computerised ledger. As stated, the Instant Accounting Journal follows double-entry bookkeeping principles, i.e., the value of the credit transaction must equal the value of the debit transaction. Each line of the Journal Entry table represents a single transaction, therefore there must be at least two transactions in the journal (a credit and a debit).

However, this does not mean that you must post a single credit item for every single debit item. You can, for example, post several debits but only one balancing credit, and vice versa. Provided the net difference between your postings is always zero (i.e. the total value of credits equals the total value of debits), you can then post the Journal.

Making a Journal Entry

For a journal entry, VAT is neither calculated for you nor posted to the VAT control account.

Here is an example of how you would make a journal entry for a transfer of funds from your business bank deposit account to your business building society account.

1 From the Nominal Ledger toolbar, click Journal.

2 Use the Calendar button if a different date is required.

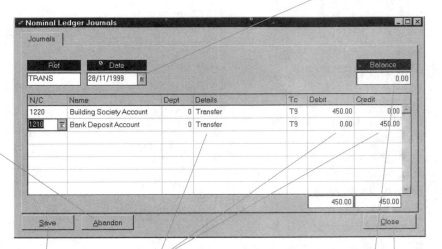

If you make a mistake simply click on the Abandon button and start again.

3 Enter details for both the credit and debit transactions. The Ref. entry is optional.

4 Note, the default Tax code of T9 is entered for you by Instant Accounting.

5 Check total Debit and Credit are equal and a zero balance is displayed in the Balance box.

6 Click Save to process your journal or Abandon to cancel.

7 Click Close to return to Nominal Ledger window.

Before saving the Journal, always ensure the Balance box shows zero. If the value of the credit transactions does not equal the value of the debit transactions, then Sage Instant Accounting issues a warning and will not let you save the Journal.

Note – Instant Accounting will not automatically calculate VAT or post it to the VAT Control Account. If VAT is required, enter each VAT element as a separate line, with a debit or credit to the appropriate VAT Control Account.

Dealing with Late Entries

Use Monthly Accruals where you are expecting a Purchase Invoice but have not received it before you are ready to perform the Month End procedure. By accruing the value of the invoice it will appear in your Profit and Loss Account, Balance Sheet and VAT Return. After completing your month end and when you receive the invoice in the next month you can reverse the accrual and post the invoice correctly (Page 63).

From time to time you will receive Purchase Invoices after you have already completed your month end procedures. These transactions are called Late Entries and, depending on how far you are through these procedures, can be dealt with in one of two ways.

- Where you have not yet completed your Profit and Loss, Balance Sheet and VAT Return and you know the value of these invoices, then you can accrue the values. Then when the invoice is received in the next month you can reverse the accrual and post the invoice correctly. This is called Monthly Accruals.

- If you have already completed your Profit and Loss, Balance Sheet and VAT Return and an invoice is subsequently received, this invoice can be posted as a late entry.

Monthly Accruals

Use journal entries to post monthly accruals as follows:

1 from the Nominal Ledger toolbar, click Journals.

2 Enter the date that appears on your Purchase Invoice.

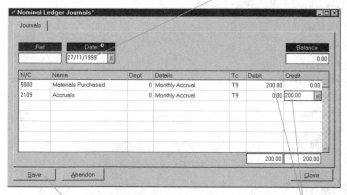

You must enter the correct date for your accrual, i.e., the same date that appears on your purchase invoice, to ensure that your VAT Return will be correct.

4 Check the date and figures then click Save.

3 Enter these journal entry details, using your actual invoice value for the Debit and Credit values here.

5 Now complete your Month End.

...cont'd

If you have received more than one late Purchase Invoice, post separate monthly accruals for each one (Page 62, Steps 1–5). Then, when you receive the invoices, reverse each accrual and post each invoice correctly.

Reversing your monthly accrual and posting your invoice correctly

After completing your month end procedures and receiving the Purchase Invoice in the next month, reverse the accrual and make a correct invoice posting as follows:

1 From the Nominal Ledger toolbar, click Journals.

2 Enter the date used when the accrual was posted.

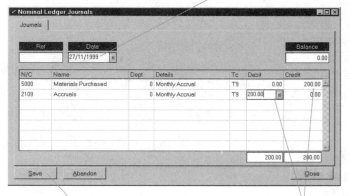

You can post more than one invoice in one go by repeating Step 7 for each late Purchase Invoice received.

4 Check the date and figures then click Save.

5 You have now reversed your monthly accruals.

3 Enter these journal entry details, using your actual invoice value for the Debit and Credit values here.

6 From the main toolbar select Suppliers, then click Invoice.

7 Type your Purchase Invoice details accurately here.

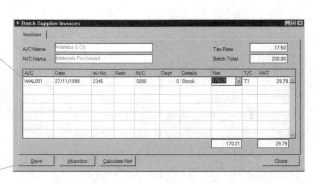

When you click Save, the details are posted instantly to update the Nominal Ledger and the relevant supplier's details.

8 Click Save, then Close.

Use Late Entry transactions where a Purchase Invoice is received after you have already completed your month end procedures and finalised your Balance Sheet, Profit and Loss and VAT Return for the month.

You can enter the late Purchase Invoice details as a whole item or enter each invoice item separately if your accounting needs to be more detailed.

If you enter each invoice item separately, always check that the final totals correctly match the invoice totals.

Late Entries

If you have already completed all of your month end procedures and then subsequently receive an invoice, it must be posted as a Late Entry. This consists of:

- Posting the Purchase Invoice using the correct tax point date, i.e., the date on the original invoice.

- Posting a journal entry for the value of the Purchase Invoice to reverse the value from your previous month's accounts.

- Posting a journal entry using a date that will record the value of the Purchase Invoice in your current month's financial reports.

To post your Purchase Invoice do the following:

1 From the Suppliers window click Invoice to bring up the Batch Supplier Invoices window.

2 Type the supplier's account code here or use the Finder button.

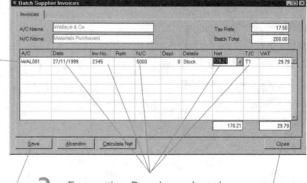

3 Enter the Purchase Invoice date and other details here.

4 When all details are correct and all invoices have been entered, click Save to post the details.

5 Click Close to return to the Suppliers window, then Close again.

...cont'd

Always check the details you have entered are correct before saving the journal entries. This avoids costly errors and ensures your financial reports are accurate.

Now you have posted the Purchase Invoice you received late you need to post a journal entry to remove the value of this purchase invoice from last month's accounts:

1 From the Nominal Ledger toolbar, click Journals.

2 Enter the date used when you posted the invoice.

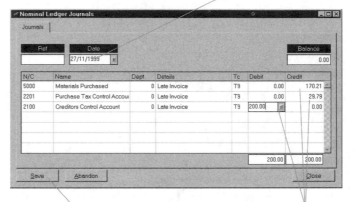

4 Check the date and figures then click Save.

3 Enter these journal entry details, using your actual invoice value here.

You need to complete the three stages of dealing with Late Entries accurately so that the accounts for both the previous month and the current month correctly reflect the late Purchase Invoice. If recorded correctly, the next time you run your financial reports for your current month, the invoice value will be included.

Having removed the value of the late invoice from your previous month's accounts, you now need to post an entry to record this value in your current month's accounts:

1 In the Nominal Ledger Journals windows, enter a date in your current month.

2 Enter these journal details, using your actual invoice values here.

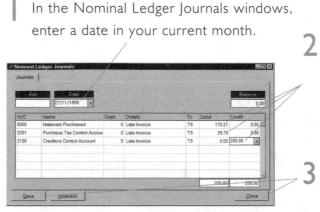

3 Check details and click Save, then Close.

The Chart of Accounts

The Chart of Accounts is subdivided into the following default report category types:

Profit and Loss

– Sales

– Purchases

– Direct Expenses

– Overheads.

Balance Sheet

– Fixed Assets

– Current Assets

– Current Liabilities

– Long Term Liabilities

– Capital and Reserves.

During installation, Instant Accounting created a simple Chart of Accounts suitable for standard reporting, such as Profit and Loss, Balance Sheet, Budget and Prior Year.

It may be that the default account names are not suitable for your business, so the Chart of Accounts can be customised to meet your business requirements. New categories types can be introduced into the accounts or current categories edited to reflect, for example, the actual items sold within your business.

1 To examine the Chart of Accounts' facilities, click COA from the Nominal Ledger window.

2 If you want to look at a chart, select it from the list and click Edit.

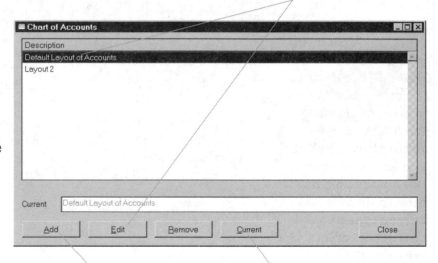

Every time you run your financial reports, you can select another layout if you wish.

Check that the name of the layout you selected appears automatically in the 'Current' text box.

3 To create a new Chart of Accounts, click the Add button.

5 When finished, click Close to return to the Nominal Ledger window.

4 To use a particular Chart of Accounts simply highlight it from the list and click the Current button.

...cont'd

If you elected to create your own chart of accounts during the Startup Wizard, the default chart of accounts will not contain any category accounts.

When you run your financial reports the value of each nominal account within each category account will be added together.

When entering nominal account ranges in Low/High boxes, type the same number in both boxes if only one code exists.

Use the Check button to find any nominal account errors in your new layout.

Creating a Chart of Accounts Layout

If you need to add a new Chart of Accounts layout, do the following:

1 Click COA from the Nominal Ledger window.

2 Click the Add button in the Chart of Accounts window.

3 Enter the name of your new Chart of Accounts layout.

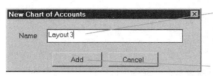

4 Click Add to continue.

5 Click on a category and change its description to that required in your financial reports.

6 Enter (or amend) the headings for each range of nominal accounts in the selected category.

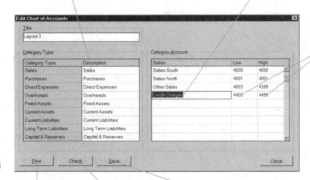

7 Set range of nominal accounts to be included for each selected category in Low and High boxes.

8 Click Check to see if you've made any errors.

9 Click Save, or Close to abandon.

10 To print your Chart of Accounts, click Print.

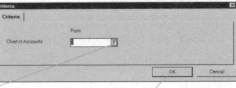

11 Select required chart in the Criteria box.

12 Click OK to print.

Nominal Reports

Also use the Nominal Reports window to delete a report, or if you need to create or edit reports.

To print or preview reports using the nominal data already entered into the system, use the Reports option from the Nominal Ledger. Sage Instant Accounting already supplies a number of pre-installed reports to suit most needs, but you can create additional custom reports using the Report Designer. See Chapter Ten for more details on creating reports.

To print a Nominal Ledger report do the following:

1 From the Nominal Ledger toolbar, click Reports.

Use the Criteria button on the Nominal Ledger window to make report generation easier by restricting the selection of nominal account codes to specified criteria.

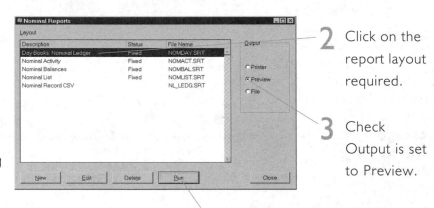

2 Click on the report layout required.

3 Check Output is set to Preview.

4 Click Run to bring up the Criteria box.

5 Type range details or use the Calendar and Finder buttons.

You may sometimes find it easier to select nominal accounts from the Nominal Ledger window instead of entering them in the Criteria box.

6 Click OK to preview the report.

7 If a printout is required click on the Print button.

8 Click Close to return to the Layout window.

9 Close all windows to finish.

The Bank

This chapter shows you how to maintain your bank account records and transactions. This includes deposits, payments, transfer of money between bank accounts and adjustments to show bank charges and interest received. It also covers reconciling your statements, processing recurring entries and producing bank statements and reports.

Covers

Chapter Six

The Bank Toolbar

This toolbar provides features for the recording and maintenance of bank transactions and records. You can perform adjustments, record the transfer of monies, enter receipts, set up recurring entries and even produce statements and reports.

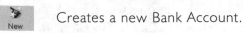 Creates a new Bank Account.

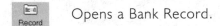 Opens a Bank Record.

 Opens Bank Account Reconciliation.

 Record Bank Payments.

 Record Supplier Payments.

 Record Money Received.

Record Customer receipts.

Make Bank Transfers.

Opens Recurring Entries Window.

To Print Bank Statements.

To Run Bank Account Reports.

Bank Accounts

To guide you through creating a new Bank account, use the New Wizard from the Bank Toolbar.

There are three types of Bank accounts used in Sage Instant Accounting: the Bank Account, Cash Account and Credit Card Account.

The Bank account option treats both Bank and Building Societies as bank accounts. Three bank accounts have been automatically set up to include a bank current account, a bank deposit account and a building society account.

A single Cash Account called Petty Cash has been set up, but other cash accounts can be added, for example, Emergency Cash or Additional Travel Expenses etc.

The arrows on the Customers toolbar let you scroll across all available buttons.

The facility to record your credit card bank details is available and allows you to monitor any credit card transactions you have made and keep track of your money. Two credit card accounts have already been set up for use.

To view the Bank account window:

Have your current bank balance to hand when creating new Bank records.

1 From the Instant Accounting Toolbar click on the Bank icon.

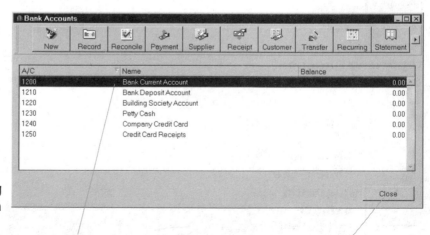

Sage Instant Accounting treats both Bank and Building Societies as Bank accounts.

2 Click once on the bank account required, then click on the appropriate icon for the function you wish to do.

3 When finished, click Close.

Bank, Cash, and Credit Card Accounts

Use the Bank Record Wizard to guide you through setting up a new bank account.

Instant Accounting provides three types of bank accounts:

- Bank Account (includes both bank deposit and current account, plus a building society account).

- Cash Account (named Petty Cash).

- Credit Card Account (company credit card and credit card receipts).

These accounts can be edited to match your own details. Accounts can also be added or deleted. To set up your Bank account details:

Refer to Chapter Eleven for more information on entering opening balances.

1 From the Bank Accounts window, select account type required and click on the Record icon.

2 Make changes if necessary here.

Your bank accounts and financial reports use nominal codes 1200 to 1299.

3 Click here to enter Current Balance. The Opening Balance Setup box appears.

4 Enter Opening Balance and other details.

5 Click Save.

6 Click Bank Details Tab and enter further details.

Should the minimum balance fall below the figure entered, it will be displayed in red in the Bank Accounts window.

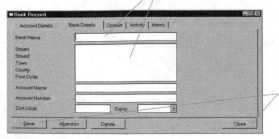

7 Click Save to store details, then Close.

Recording Bank Payments

Any payments to your suppliers should be entered using the Supplier option as this will automatically bring up any outstanding invoices when the supplier's account reference is entered.

For recording any non-invoiced or one-off payments use the Payment option from the Bank Accounts window. Sage Instant Accounting then makes it very easy for you to keep track of where your money goes – simply select the appropriate account, enter the payment and post it.

To record Bank payments:

1 Click Payment from the Bank Accounts window.

2 Use the Finder button to enter the Bank account code.

3 Enter Date and transaction Reference (if required).

If you only know the Gross value of the payment, simply enter it in the Net box and click on the Calculate Net button.

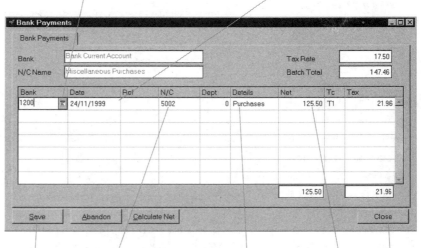

4 Enter a Nominal Code for the payment to be posted to, or use the Finder button.

5 Enter Details.

6 Enter amount (change Tax Code from default of T1 if necessary).

Use the Abandon button if you want to clear the data and start again. Any entries already saved will not be cancelled.

7 Click Save to post details (update the nominal ledger and the Bank account).

8 Click Close to finish.

Supplier Invoice Payments

Instead of using the scroll buttons on the Bank toolbar, simply point with the cursor inside the Bank Accounts window and click the right mouse button to bring up a complete list of toolbar options.

The Supplier option from the Bank Accounts toolbar will provide you with a detailed transaction list of any outstanding invoice items, credit notes and payments made on account to suppliers. To record payment of a supplier invoice do the following:

1 From the Bank Accounts window, click on type of account required (e.g., Bank Current Account) and click Supplier.

2 Enter supplier account code.

3 Use Calendar button if payment date is different.

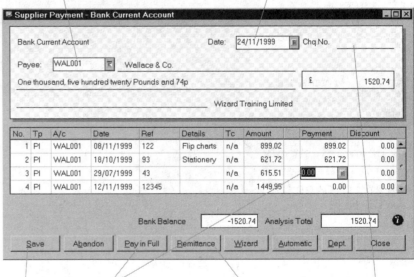

Enter a discount value in the discount box, not a percentage, for any invoiced item. The Analysis Total box decreases by the discount value entered.

5 Enter value in Payment box for part-payment or click on Pay in Full button to enter full amount.

4 Enter cheque number, if required for reference.

6 Repeat Step 5 for any remaining transactions.

7 Click Remittance button to print remittance.

You don't have to enter a value in the cheque box: Instant Accounting does it for you.

8 Click Save to save payment details and Close.

Bank Receipts

If you accept payment for goods and services by credit card, deposit a batch of credit card vouchers into your appropriate Bank account, i.e., Company Credit Card Receipts.

To record any non-invoiced or miscellaneous money you receive, the Receipts option from the Bank Accounts window is used. These items are allocated a specific nominal code for analysis purposes so a check can be made on monies received.

To enter receipt of money:

1 From the Bank Account window Click on the Receipt icon.

2 In the Bank Receipts window, select the appropriate Bank account.

3 Ensure the required Date is entered here.

4 Enter a Reference here, such as a cheque number.

If you only have the Gross value to hand, enter it in the Net box and click on Calculate Net.

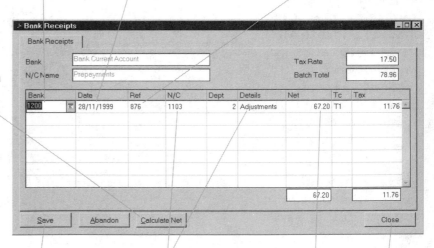

Batch Total is the sum of Net and Tax totals (i.e., Gross).

5 Select a Nominal Account Code to post the receipt to and give details.

6 Enter Net value.

A receipt reference, i.e., cheque number or deposit number, will help when reconciling bank accounts.

7 Repeat Steps 2–6 to record further receipts, then click Save to post transactions.

8 When finished, Close all windows.

Recording Customer Receipts

First enter the gross amount received in the Amount box, then check to ensure this equals the Analysis Total when you have finished.

The Customer option from the Bank Accounts window is used to record money received from your customers. When the customer's account reference is entered, any outstanding invoices appear automatically in the Customer Receipt window.

To record full payments:

1 From the Bank Accounts window, select the bank account required and click Customer.

Use the Customers Receipt Wizard to help you record invoice payments by cheque, allocate all credit notes and payments on account to invoices or post a payment on account only.

2 Enter a customer Account Code to display all items not fully paid for that customer.

3 Change Date if necessary and enter a paying in Reference if possible.

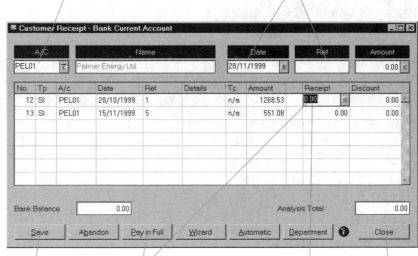

You can pay an invoice in full or part but you cannot allocate an amount more than the item value.

If there are no out-standing transactions then no items will be displayed.

4 If FULL payment has been received, select a transaction and click Pay in Full.

5 If this is a PART payment, enter the amount received here.

6 Enter any further receipts then click Save to process them or Abandon to start again.

7 When finished Close all windows.

Bank Transfers

There is also a Wizard to help you make a Bank Transfer.

Sometimes you will need to transfer money from one bank account to another. You can record this using the Transfer option from the Bank Accounts window or by making a journal entry.

To make a bank transfer do the following:

You can also record a Bank Transfer through a journal entry.

1 From the Bank Accounts window, select the bank account you wish to move the money from.

2 Click Transfer to bring up the Bank Transfer window.

The Reference details will be recorded in the Audit Trail. You are allowed up to eight characters.

4 Enter a Reference and appropriate Details.

3 Enter the Nominal Code of the Bank account you are transferring to.

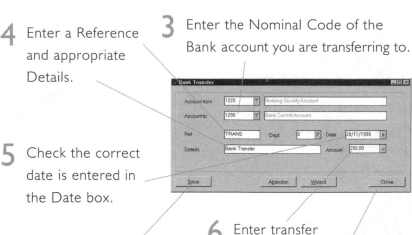

5 Check the correct date is entered in the Date box.

Instant Accounting always enters today's date in the Date box, but this can be altered if necessary.

6 Enter transfer amount.

7 Click Save to process transfer or Abandon to start again.

8 Click Close to finish, then Close again.

Recurring Entries

Recurring entries need processing each month before you can run the Month or Year End procedures.

For payments which remain consistent and are paid on a monthly basis, for example rent and electricity, the Recurring option can be used from the Bank Accounts window. This feature is also useful for standing orders and direct debits and prevents payments such as these from being overlooked. Each month, these transactions need posting to update your banks and ledgers.

If there are any outstanding recurring entries, you will be reminded to post them. To add a recurring entry:

Instant Accounting will only let you post journal credits when you post journal debits of the same value, and vice versa.

1 Select Recurring from the Bank Accounts window and Click Add.

2 Enter transaction type from the list box.

3 Enter the Bank Account Code.

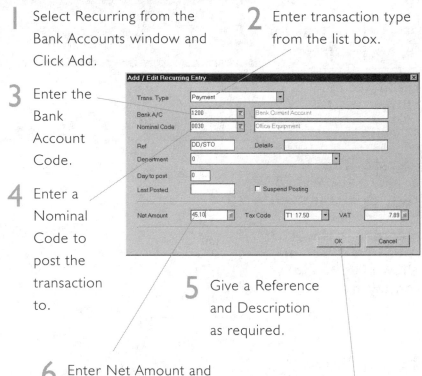

4 Enter a Nominal Code to post the transaction to.

The Last Posted box will remain blank until the new entry is saved and processed.

5 Give a Reference and Description as required.

To stop a monthly payment, click the Suspend Posting box. This is handy for some payments which do not need posting every month.

6 Enter Net Amount and check the Tax Code.

7 Click OK to return to the Recurring Entries window.

8 Click Process and Process All to process the recurring entries, click Close to finish.

The Bank Statement

Sage Instant Accounting provides you with the facility to print your bank statements out at any time, showing all reconciled bank payments and receipts.

These statements show the transactions made to and from each bank account, and prove useful for cross-referencing purposes when checking for any transaction omissions or additions. To print a report in bank statement format do the following:

To use this facility effectively, you should make sure that you enter all Bank transactions accurately and completely so that the Sage Instant Accounting Bank statements match your actual bank statements.

1 From the Bank Accounts window click on the Statement button to bring up the Criteria window.

2 Enter Transaction Date range.

3 Enter To and From Bank Ref. using Finder button for ease.

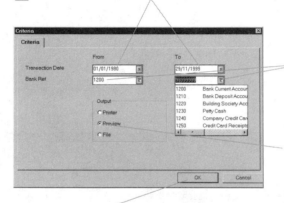

You can also save the Bank Statement reports as a file for use at a later date. Simply click on the Save As button in the report preview window.

4 Select Preview from Output options.

5 Click Run to preview statement.

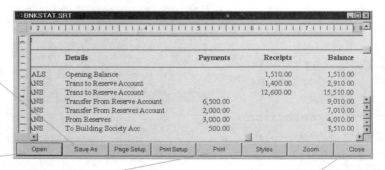

To bring up previously saved statements, Click Open and select the required statement from the list.

6 Click Print and OK from the print dialog box.

7 Click Close to return to Bank Accounts window.

Bank Activity

To change the range of transactions that are shown, choose the range button. This allows you to specify an audit trail number or a date range.

Sage Instant Accounting allows you to view the transactions you have made within your bank accounts. This is useful if you need to query a bank transfer or purchase payment made at some time during the financial year.

The activity screen will initially list all of the transactions you have made in a bank account, but if you know the approximate date when the transaction you are looking for was made, you can limit the transactions displayed by specifying a date range. You can also limit the display by entering an audit trail number range.

Follow these easy steps to view bank activity:

1 From the Sage Instant Accounting toolbar click on the Bank icon.

2 In the Bank Accounts window click on the Bank account you want to view to highlight it, then click on the Record button.

3 Select the Activity tab.

Use the Tidy button to clear all transaction sub-items from view.

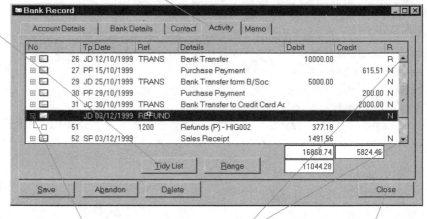

The codes identifying the transaction type are the same as those used in the Audit Trail.

4 Double-click on a transaction for more details (where available).

5 Use the scroll arrows to move through the transactions.

6 Close all windows when finished.

...cont'd

 If the Date Range is not too different from that already displayed, instead of entering the full date from the keyboard simply click in the appropriate date box and use the up or down keyboard cursor keys to increment or decrement one day at a time.

 The 'No' column shows the Audit Trail number which is assigned to each transaction automatically by Sage Instant Accounting.

 The 'R' column shows whether or not a transaction has been reconciled with the bank, where

R = Reconciled and
N = Not Reconciled.

Specifying a Range

To limit the transactions displayed you can specify a date range. For example, to display only transactions in November 1999 do the following:

1 In the Bank Record Activity window, click Range.

2 Enter the From and To Date Range here.

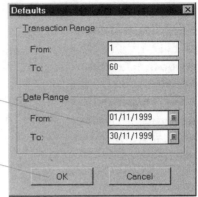

3 Click OK.

4 The Bank Record Activity window displays only transactions in November 1999.

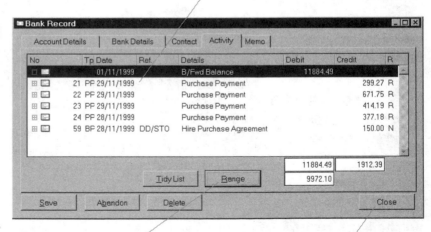

5 Click the Range button and specify a new range if required.

6 When finished click Close, then Close the Bank Accounts window.

Bank Account Reconciliation

Before you select any transactions to reconcile, always check that the opening balance shown in the Bank Reconciliation window is the same as the opening balance on your actual bank statement.

Bank reconciliation is the process of matching up your computer bank records and transactions with those shown on your bank statements.

The Bank Reconciliation window displays transactions which have not been previously reconciled. After entering the date of the statement, you can work through your bank statement matching the transactions recorded in Sage Instant Accounting. If necessary, you should make any adjustments needed to ensure that the Instant Accounting bank accounts accurately reflect the transactions processed by your actual bank. To reconcile a bank account:

1 From the Bank Accounts window select the bank account to be reconciled, then click Reconcile.

Refer to the F1 help key or the Library for additional information about bank reconciliation.

2 Enter date of actual bank statement and press Tab.

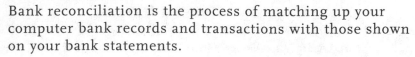

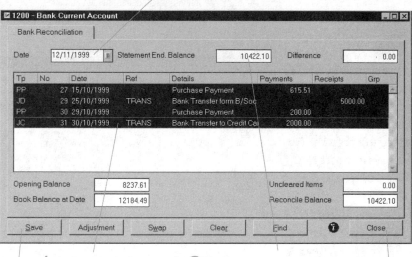

A bank account cannot be reconciled if the check box No Bank Reconciliation has been selected on the bank record.

4 Click on each transaction that matches on your bank statement.

3 Enter closing balance of your actual bank statement in the Statement End Balance box.

To search for specific transactions use the Find button.

5 If the Reconcile and Statement End balances match, click Save.

6 Click Close.

...cont'd

Thoroughly check all transactions on the bank statement against the Bank Reconciliation list. Check that the Reconcile Balance box matches the closing balance of your bank statement.

Bank reconciliation will only work correctly provided that a number of important rules are followed:

• The opening balance shown on the Bank Reconciliation window must match the opening balance on your actual bank statement

If for some reason they are different, you will need to check why and make the necessary adjustments. One way of doing this is to view the selected bank's activity from within the nominal ledger. To see if a transaction has been reconciled or not, check the Bank column in the Audit Trail, where R = reconciled and N = not reconciled.

As you select each transaction you will see the Reconcile Balance change automatically.

• Work through your actual bank statement progressively one line at a time, clicking on the corresponding transaction entry in the Bank reconciliation window to highlight it.

• If you come across a transaction on your bank statement not shown in Instant Accounting, you should record this transaction immediately using the Adjustments facility.

Use Adjustments button or Bank Payments, Receipts and Transfers to record any additional transactions shown on your bank statement, e.g., bank charges, cash point withdrawals etc.

• Check everything carefully. When you are satisfied that all necessary transactions for reconciliation have been selected and any adjustments made, the Difference box should show zero.

Making Adjustments

1 From the Reconciliation window click on the Adjustments button.

2 Enter the Nominal Code of the account to receive the adjustment.

3 Enter adjustment details.

4 If correct click Save, then Close.

Bank Reports

HOT TIP **When you have become familiar with the various reports you can save time by sending them straight to the printer without the need to preview. Select Printer instead of Preview in Step 3.**

There is a wide range of ready-to-use bank reports provided by Sage Instant Accounting. These reports outline your bank details and transactions and help you keep track of your bank finances. It is advisable that you regularly print out the standard reports, such as Day Books, once you have entered the relevant transactions.

1 From the Bank Accounts window click Reports to bring up the Bank Reports window.

2 Click on the report required.

3 Ensure Preview is selected.

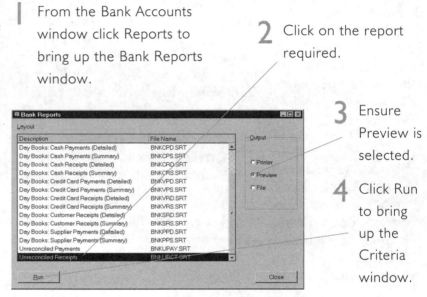

4 Click Run to bring up the Criteria window.

HOT TIP **You can save a report as a file in a number of useful formats, such as Microsoft Write, Text file or Comma Separated Value (CSV).**

5 Enter Criteria required for report.

6 Click OK to generate the report.

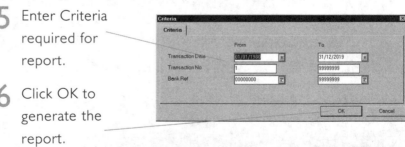

HOT TIP **If you choose to print the report, the Windows Print dialog box appears. Use this to select which pages to print and change your printer settings if necessary.**

7 Click Print, then OK and Close.

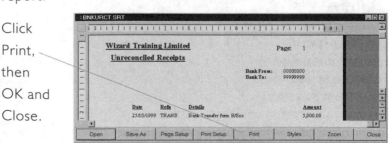

84

Products

This chapter shows you how to create and maintain records for products you buy and sell and how to set up product codes. These details, once recorded in the system, will be entered automatically for you when creating product invoices or credit notes etc. You will also learn how to produce reports documenting your product details.

Covers

Chapter Seven

The Products Toolbar

The Products toolbar provides features for the recording and maintenance of product records. New records can be created manually or by using the Product Record Wizard, whilst reports of Product lists and records can be generated as required.

 Creates a new Product Record.

 Opens a Product Record.

 To Run Product Reports.

Product Categories

For accurate analysis reporting, Sage Instant Accounting lets you divide your products into 999 categories.

Sage Instant Accounting lets you divide your products into a number of different categories, up to a maximum of 999. These categories are set up using the Product Categories option from the Settings menu and appear in the drop-down list when you click on Category in the Product Record window.

These product categories are useful for producing accurate analysis reports using the Report Designer. To edit an existing product category or simply add a new one, do the following:

You can simply double-click on a Category to bring up the Edit box.

| From the Instant Accounting menu bar, select Settings, then Product Categories.

2 Click on the Product Category you wish to change.

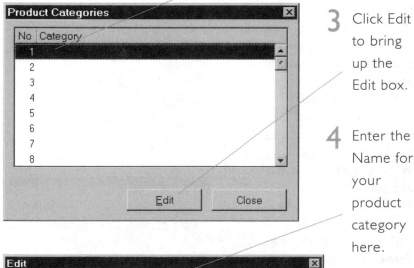

3 Click Edit to bring up the Edit box.

4 Enter the Name for your product category here.

It is not compulsory to set up different Product Categories, but it is useful to categorise your products for reporting purposes. You can then use Criteria to select a specific product range.

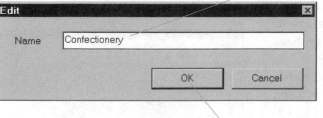

5 Click OK, then Close the Product Categories box.

The Product Record

Sage Instant Accounting allows you to divide products into 999 different categories using the Product Categories option from the Settings menu.

**There is no stock control function available with Instant Accounting. If your Business has a requirement to record movement of stock, monitor stock levels etc., then you should consider an upgrade to Sage Line 50, which features a full stock control facility and allows you to generate Sales and Purchase Orders, set up Opening Balances and track Product activity.
For more on this product, see 'Sage Line 50', also in the 'in easy steps' series.**

Sage Instant Accounting allows you to create, edit or delete records for all the products your business sells. Once these records have been set up, all you need to do is enter a product code and the details will be automatically included for you on any product invoice or credit note you create.

From the Product Record window you can view the sales price and location for each product as well as who the supplier is. Use the Products option to:

- Create and maintain records for all products bought and sold.

- Produce reports documenting your product details.

- Produce a report listing all the products on record.

The Product Record window

From the Product Record window you can view the Sales Price and Supplier for each product, together with the Product Code and Description.

1 To bring up the Products window click Products from the Instant Accounting toolbar.

2 To view Product details, select the product and click Record.

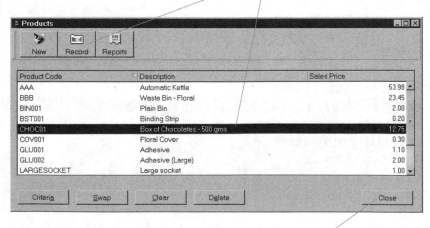

3 To finish click Close.

...cont'd

You may find it easier at first to let the Product Record Wizard create a new product record for you. Just click on the New option from the Products window.

Entering a product record

1 From the Products window click on Record.

2 Type a unique Product Code here and press Tab.

3 Enter Description.

4 Enter relevant details here.

Use the Memo tab to record any additional notes you wish to make about your products.

5 Choose a Nominal sales account for this product.

6 Select correct VAT code.

7 Enter Sales Price here.

8 Enter any remaining details on the Product Record.

9 Click Save to keep the record, or Abandon to abort.

10 Click Close to return to Products window.

You can update the sales price for all product items using the Global Changes option from the Tools menu. You can increase or decrease the price by a sum or a percentage.

Useful notes for completing product details:

Product Code	Up to 16 characters allowed, including A–Z, 0–9, /.-# but no spaces. Each different product must have its own unique code.
Supplier A/C	Use the Finder button to enter account code for the supplier of this product.
Sales Price	This is the net selling price (i.e. ex. VAT) to be used for invoices and credit notes.

Product Defaults

To save time and make the process of creating new product records easier, Sage Instant Accounting lets you set up certain product defaults.

Whenever a new product record is created certain regular details, e.g. Nominal Code, Tax Code, Department etc., are asked for. If you use a recording system where these codes remain the same for most of your products, default settings can be set up which will then appear automatically in each new product record without you having to enter them every time. You set up product defaults as follows:

1 From the Instant Accounting menu bar, select Settings, then Product Defaults.

2 Enter the Nominal Code to be used by default whenever you create product invoices.

3 Select the VAT rate code from the drop-down list box.

4 Describe the unit of sale here, e.g. 'each', 'box'.

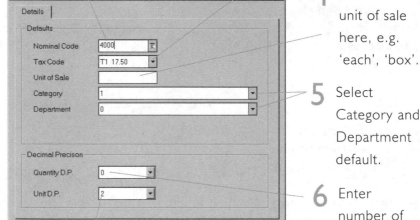

5 Select Category and Department default.

6 Enter number of decimal places for quantities.

7 Enter number of decimal places for your product sales prices.

8 Click OK to save or Cancel to abandon any changes.

Using Criteria

Use the Amounts tab to apply criteria to monetary data types, such as Sales Price and Unit of Sale.

Using criteria speeds up the process of searching for specific product records, for example to show products which match a particular description, cost range or product category. The following example shows how to set up Criteria to restrict Product Records to only those with a Sale Price of between five and ten pounds:

1 From the Products window, click on the Criteria button to bring up the Criteria window.

2 Click on the Amounts tab.

Wildcards, such as * can be used in the Value text boxes.

3 Select the check box of the data type required.

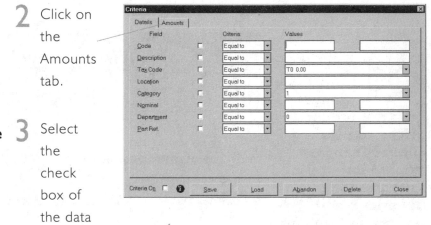

4 Select appropriate Criteria.

If you do not wish to apply criteria already entered, ensure the Criteria On check box is deselected.

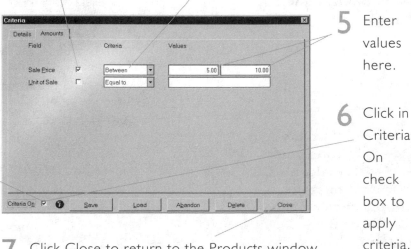

5 Enter values here.

6 Click in Criteria On check box to apply criteria.

7 Click Close to return to the Products window.

Changing Values Globally

To amend values for all, or a selected group of products within the Product Record, select the Global Changes option from the Tools menu.

The Global Changes option lets you change values within the Product Record for either all or just a selected range of products. Using the Global Changes Wizard means you can change information quickly without having to find and edit each record manually.

The following example shows you how to increase the sales price of two selected products by 3%:

1 From the Instant Accounting menu bar, select Tools, then Global Changes.

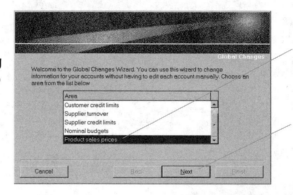

As well as for making changes to product prices, use the Global Changes Wizard for altering Customer and Supplier credit limits and turnover and for making Nominal Budget changes.

2 Select Product sales prices.

3 Click Next.

4 Highlight the type of change required.

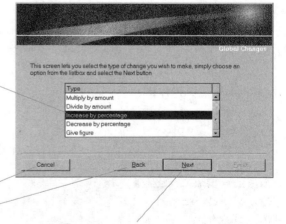

If at any time you make a mistake, simply click on the Cancel or Back button.

5 Click Next to bring up the next Wizard screen.

...cont'd

The value entered will be limited by the default Unit DP entered for Step 7 on Page 90.

6 Enter the percentage value to increase the price by here.

7 Click Next.

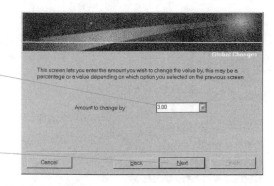

You may find it useful to use the Swap or Clear buttons when making your selection here.

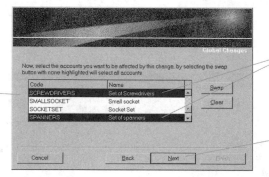

8 Click on the items you want to be affected by the change.

9 Click Next to continue.

10 Check the details for your changes to ensure they are correct.

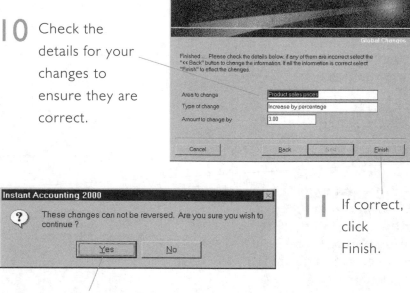

Always make sure that you have entered the correct information before confirming the changes. Once implemented, they cannot be automatically reversed.

11 If correct, click Finish.

12 Click Yes to confirm changes.

Product Reports

The Product Reports option allows you to print out useful pre-prepared product related reports. These reports show such things as product details and can be tailored to your needs by specifying a criteria range, provided these details have been entered at the product record stage.

Additional product reports tailored to your business needs can be created using the Report Designer (see Chapter Ten). To run a Product Report:

Use the Criteria button on the Products window when you need to select specific ranges of products to report on.

You can also save the report as a file, i.e., Text file (.TXT) or Comma Separated Variable (.CSV).

If you selected to print the report, the Windows Print dialog box appears. Use this to select which pages to print and change your printer settings if necessary.

1 From the Products window click Reports to bring up the Product Reports list.

2 Click on the report you require.

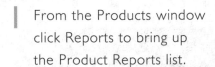

3 Ensure Preview is selected.

4 Click Run to bring up the Criteria window.

5 Enter Criteria required for report.

6 Click OK to generate report.

7 Click Print, then OK and Close.

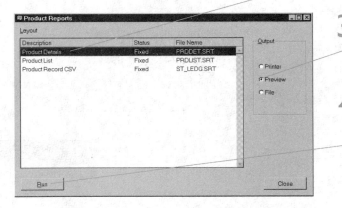

Invoices

This chapter shows you how to produce invoices and credit notes for your products and services. Customers, Products and Nominal Accounts are directly linked to Invoicing so the invoices produced automatically update the relevant ledgers. Any raised invoices not posted or printed can be easily and quickly monitored.

Covers

Chapter Eight

The Invoicing Toolbar

This toolbar provides facilities for generating invoices and credit notes for the goods you sell and the services you provide. Ledgers can be automatically updated, transactions printed out and a number of reports generated for analysis purposes.

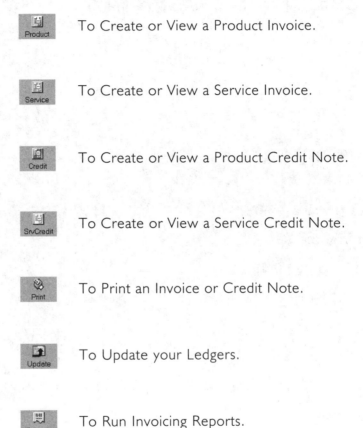

To Create or View a Product Invoice.

To Create or View a Service Invoice.

To Create or View a Product Credit Note.

To Create or View a Service Credit Note.

To Print an Invoice or Credit Note.

To Update your Ledgers.

To Run Invoicing Reports.

Invoicing

Sage Instant Accounting generates invoice numbers in sequence, normally starting at 1. However, you can start with your own numbering system, of up to seven digits. This will be incremented for you each time a new invoice is generated.

As you create invoices they are displayed in the Invoicing list box, one line per invoice. Product details are automatically pulled into the Invoice from the Instant Accounting Product records.

Invoices remain in the Invoicing window list box until removed using the Delete option.

Processing manually generated invoices, or batch invoicing, has already been referred to in Chapters Three and Four. Briefly, Chapter Three (Customers) explains how to log invoices and credit notes within the system after they have been produced and sent to customers. Chapter Four (Suppliers) explains how to record invoices and credit notes you receive from your suppliers.

Invoicing deals with Sage Instant Accounting generated invoices, of which there are two basic types. Firstly there is the Product Invoice, which is used for invoicing customers for the products you sell. Each line of the invoice can be used for recording specific product items. Early discount settlement can be offered on these invoices and carriage charges applied.

Meanwhile the Service Invoice is used to invoice customers you have provided a service for. An unlimited amount of text can be entered into the invoice describing the services supplied. As with the Product Invoice, discount settlement can be applied and carriage charges recorded.

Because Sage Instant Accounting generates these invoices, all the relevant details are automatically recorded and posted for you when you are ready. You have the option of posting each line of the invoice to a separate nominal account or posting the total value of the invoice to a single nominal account.

You can also add further details to your invoice, such as a customer order number. Should you have already received full or part payment for the invoice, you can allocate that payment to the invoice as you create it.

Within Invoicing you can also generate credit notes for your customers, to cater for products or services that have not been received or had to be returned. As these are posted, the ledgers will be updated automatically.

You do, of course, need to keep track of your invoicing and should use the report facility regularly to print out a list of Invoices not yet printed or posted.

The Product Invoice

To retrieve and edit an existing invoice simply select the invoice from the Invoicing window and click Product.

To invoice your customers for the products you sell, use the Product option from the Invoicing toolbar. Be careful not to confuse this button with the Products icon on the Sage Instant Accounting toolbar. To create an Invoice click Invoicing on the main toolbar, then do the following:

As well as normal product codes, you can also enter special non-product codes:

S1 = Non-product item with price and VAT amount.

S2 = Non-product item, exempt for VAT (Tax code T0).

M = Non-product item with additional message, no price or VAT amount.

1 Click Product from the Invoicing toolbar.

2 Enter the tax point date if different from current date.

3 Type a Sales Order No. if applicable here.

4 Enter Customer Account Code.

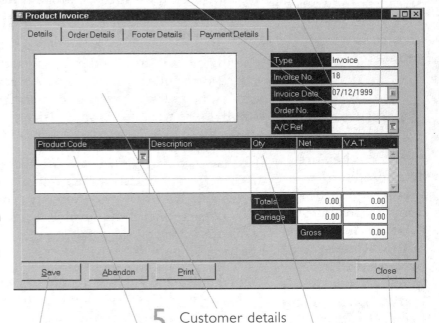

5 Customer details appear here.

Use the message box (Product Code M) to add any text in the main body of the invoice.

6 Enter the Product Code here (use Finder button).

7 Enter Quantity here.

8 Repeat Steps 6 and 7 for further products, then click Save to finish.

9 Click Close.

...cont'd

If you selected Invoices default to Account Reference in the Invoices Defaults dialog box, the cursor will always appear in the A/C Ref box when you click to create a new invoice. Use the Shift+Tab keys as an alternative to clicking with the mouse to move up to the Invoice No. box.

You can edit the address of the account once it appears on the invoice. The changes will not be recorded in the Customer record.

If you need to edit an existing invoice, simply enter its number in the Invoice No. box and press the Tab key to display it.

Entering Invoice Details

The previous page shows you the Invoice Details dialog box and how and where to enter these details. Here are some important notes to follow when creating an Invoice (or Credit Note):

Type	Confirms this is an Invoice and cannot be altered by the user.
Invoice No.	This will display 1 the very first time you create an invoice. You can start with this number or change it if your business already has its own numbering system. You are allowed up to seven digits. Whatever number you choose to start from, Instant Accounting will then automatically generate all subsequent invoice numbers in sequence for you.
Invoice Date	This is where you enter the tax point date of the invoice.
Order No.	Use this to record your order number.
A/C Ref	This identifies the customer account for the invoice. When entered, Instant Accounting automatically brings up the customer name and address on the invoice. If you enter an account not already set up, Instant accounting invokes the Finder so you can either select another account or create a new one using the New button.
Description	When you enter a product code in the Product Code box, Instant Accounting automatically enters a description here, taken from the Product record. You can edit this description if you wish.
Qty	When you enter the quantity of stock sold here, Instant Accounting automatically completes the Net and VAT boxes for you.

Any changes made to the delivery details are not saved back to the Customer Record.

Product Invoice Order Details

You can record useful additional Order Details on your Invoice if necessary:

1 Click on Order Details tab.

2 Enter Delivery Address.

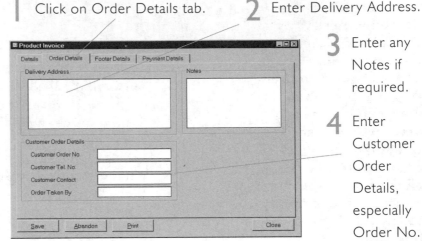

3 Enter any Notes if required.

4 Enter Customer Order Details, especially Order No.

Using the Footer Details tab you can enter or amend any settlement terms, and add any analysis conditions that you wish to apply to the entire invoice, e.g. the Tax Code, Nominal Account Code and Department.

Product Invoice Footer Details

Further details, such as Carriage and Settlement Terms, go in the Footer Details:

5 Click on Footer Details tab.

6 Enter any Carriage details here.

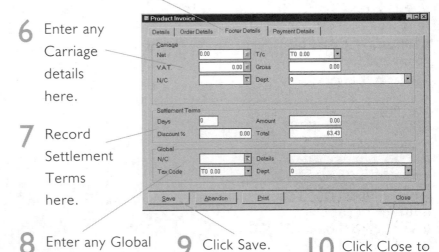

7 Record Settlement Terms here.

For a payment which has already been received and can be allocated against a product invoice, record it using the Payment Details tab.

8 Enter any Global detail changes.

9 Click Save.

10 Click Close to finish.

You can enter a full or a part payment in the Payment Amount box. Use the Calculator button to help calculate the amount.

Product Invoice Payment Details

You can record any advance payment you have already received for the invoice as you create it:

1 Click on the Payment Details tab.

2 Enter a reference which relates to the payment.

3 Enter code of bank the money is to be paid to.

4 Payment Amount goes here.

If you select the Post as Payment on Account option, you must then use the Customer Receipt function from the Bank option to allocate it.

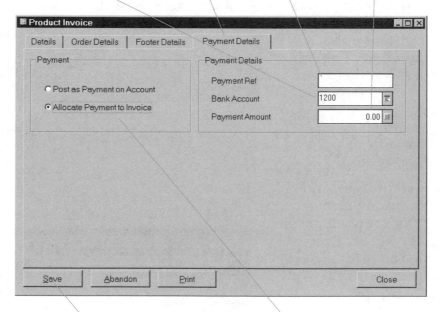

You cannot enter a value in the Payment Amount box that exceeds the value of the invoice.

6 Click Save, then Close.

5 Select to Post as Payment on Account or to Allocate Payment to Invoice.

When you post the invoice by selecting the Update option from the Invoicing toolbar, the payment will be recorded and deducted from the invoice total.

If the Payment Amount is the full amount of the invoice, the payment will be automatically allocated to the invoice.

If the Payment Amount is less than the invoice amount, the invoice will be part paid.

Printing an Invoice

When using the Invoicing option to create invoices and credit notes, you can choose either to print straight away or save them as a batch for printing later using the Print option on the Invoicing Toolbar.

Sage Instant Accounting gives you the option to print Invoices or Credit Notes either immediately, or at a later date. To print straight away after you have entered all of the details, instead of clicking Save do the following:

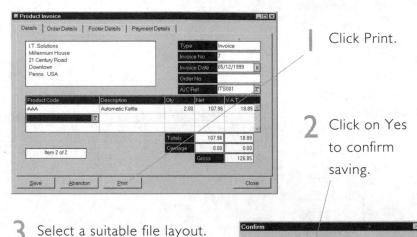

1 Click Print.

2 Click on Yes to confirm saving.

Batching invoices or credit notes is useful if you only have one printer. You simply load the correct stationery in the printer once, then print them all in one go.

3 Select a suitable file layout.

4 Check Output is set to Printer.

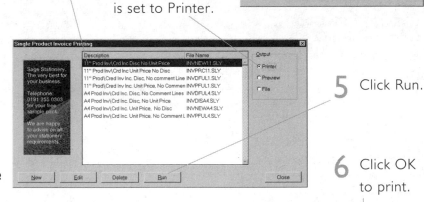

5 Click Run.

6 Click OK to print.

If no records are selected from the list in the Invoicing window, all non-printed invoices or credit notes will be printed.

7 Select Preview then click OK.

8 Click Close to finish.

The Service Invoice

Sage Instant Accounting warns you if a selected customer account has been marked as 'on hold' on the Customer Record.

To invoice customers for the services you provide instead of products you sell, you should generate a Service Invoice using the Service button from the Invoicing Toolbar. An unlimited amount of text can be entered to describe the services provided, and each service can be analysed to a different nominal account. Settlement discounts can also be applied as well as recording carriage charges.

As with Product Invoices, a Service Invoice can be saved to print in a batch later or printed straight away. At this point you have the option to update the ledgers at the same time or leave until a more appropriate time.

1 Click Service from the Invoicing toolbar.

2 Type correct date if different from current date.

3 Enter Order Number.

4 Enter Customer Code.

Select a service item and click on the Edit box or Press F3 to view item details. If required, you can alter the Posting Details or edit the Details text.

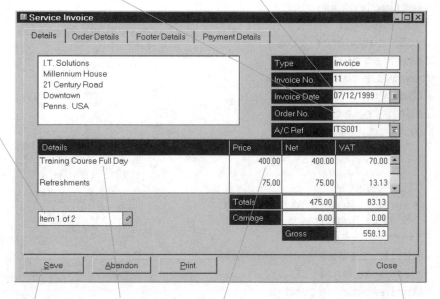

5 Type service Details here.

6 Enter net Price.

7 Repeat Steps 5 and 6 as required.

If you make a mistake, simply click Abandon and start again.

8 Click Save to print later, or Print to print now.

9 Click Close to finish.

...cont'd

Any changes made to the delivery details are not saved back to the Customer Record.

Using the Footer Details tab you can enter or amend any settlement terms you operate with your customer. You can also add any analysis conditions that you wish to apply to the entire invoice.

For payments you have received which can be allocated against the invoice, record the details using the Payment Details tab.

Service Invoice Order Details
You can record useful additional Order Details on your Service Invoice if required:

1 Click on Order Details tab.

2 Enter Delivery Address.

3 Enter any Notes if required.

4 Enter Customer Order Details, such as Order No.

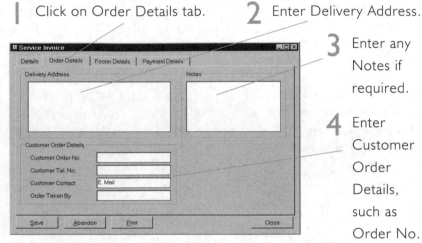

Service Invoice Footer Details
You can record details such as Carriage and Settlement Terms in the Footer Details box:

5 Click on Footer Details tab.

6 Enter any Carriage details here.

7 Record Settlement Terms here.

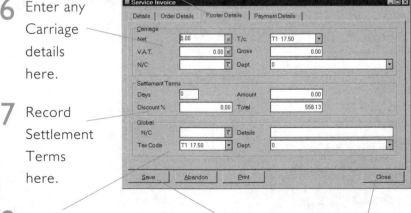

8 Enter any Global detail changes.

9 Click Save.

10 Click Close to finish.

...cont'd

You can enter a full or a part payment in the Payment Amount box. Use the Calculator button to help calculate the amount.

A quick way to alter the date in a Date box is to use the up or down cursor keys to move through the days. Pressing Page Up or Page Down moves through the months.

You cannot enter a value in the Payment Amount box that exceeds the value of the invoice.

Service Invoice Payment Details

You can record any advance payment you have already received for the invoice as you create it:

1 Click on the Payment Details tab.

2 Enter a reference which relates to the payment.

3 Enter code of bank the money is to be paid to.

4 Payment Amount goes here.

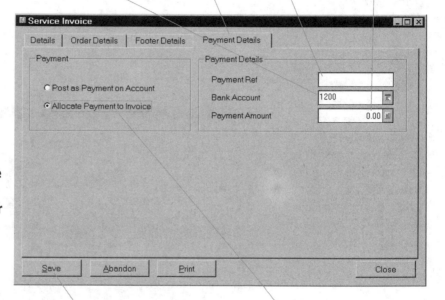

6 Click Save, then Close.

5 Select to Post as Payment on Account or to Allocate Payment to Invoice.

When you post the invoice by selecting the Update option from the Invoicing toolbar, the payment will be recorded and deducted from the invoice total.

If the Payment Amount is the full amount of the invoice, the payment will be automatically allocated to the invoice.

If the Payment Amount is less than the invoice amount, the invoice will be part paid.

Product Credit Note

The Net and VAT boxes are auto-matically calculated for you using the quantity of the product and the sales price (including any discount).

From time to time goods sent to customers may be returned as faulty, past an expiry date etc., or the customer may simply have been overcharged by mistake.

Instead of correcting the original invoice, a Product Credit Note can be issued to the Customer, detailing the amount owing to them. When your ledgers are updated, the necessary postings will be made to reflect this amendment. Do the following to create a Product Credit Note:

1 Click Credit from the Invoicing toolbar.

2 Enter date for the credit note if different from current date.

3 Type your Order No. if applicable here.

4 Enter Customer Account Code.

The first time you create a credit note, Instant Accounting starts the numbering from 1 but you can use your own number system if you wish (up to 7 digits).

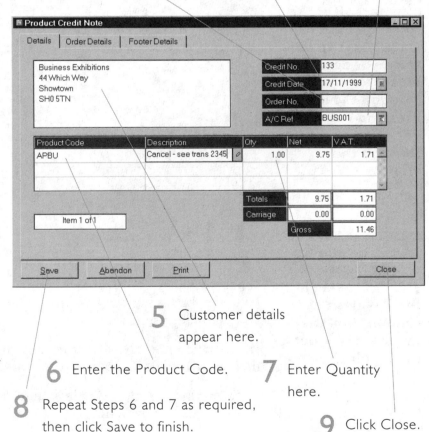

5 Customer details appear here.

One-off details can be entered against each Credit Note product item to record, for example, changes to customer discounts, address, unit price or simply to add a short comment.

6 Enter the Product Code.

7 Enter Quantity here.

8 Repeat Steps 6 and 7 as required, then click Save to finish.

9 Click Close.

Service Credit Note

A Service Credit Note can be used where, for example, customers have been charged or overcharged for a service they have not received. In this case you would issue a Service Credit Note detailing the changes made and the amount owing to the customer. When the ledgers are updated, the necessary postings will be made.

This method replaces editing the original service invoice and regenerating a new one:

A VAT only credit note can be raised where a customer has been invoiced and charged tax for goods which are exempt from VAT.

1 Click SrvCredit from the Invoicing toolbar.

2 Type correct date if different from current date.

3 Enter Order Number.

4 Enter Customer Code.

To edit an existing credit note, enter the credit note number in the Credit No. box and press TAB.

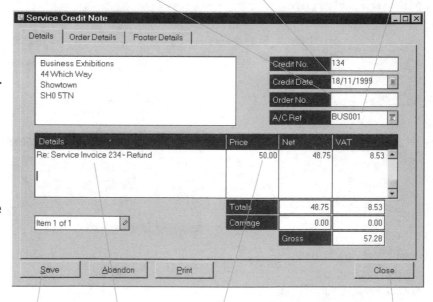

Service Credit Note

| Details | Order Details | Footer Details |

Business Exhibitions
44 Which Way
Showtown
SH0 5TN

Credit No. 134
Credit Date 18/11/1999
Order No.
A/C Ref BUS001

Details	Price	Net	VAT
Re: Service Invoice 234 - Refund	50.00	48.75	8.53

Item 1 of 1

	Net	VAT
Totals	48.75	8.53
Carriage	0.00	0.00
Gross	57.28	

Save   Abandon   Print   Close

Choose the Save button to save the credit note for printing later in a 'batch'. To print the credit note straight away and update the ledgers, choose the Print button instead.

5 Type service credit Details here.

6 Enter the Price of refund.

7 Repeat Steps 5 and 6 as required.

8 Click Save to print later, or Print to print now.

9 Click Close to finish.

Updating your Ledgers

After Updating, you can view the changes to the customer ledger and stock by using the Activity option.

Use the Clear button to deselect all before starting.

You cannot update an invoice or credit note more than once to the ledgers.

Always make sure you select at least one Invoice or Credit Note before using the Update function otherwise Sage Instant Accounting will ask you if you want to process ALL non-posted invoices and credit notes.

After creating your invoices and credit notes, the Update function is used to transfer the appropriate details to the customer and nominal ledgers.

Sage Instant Accounting gives you the option to print the update report immediately, preview it first so that you can select only certain pages for printing, or to save the report as a file so you can retrieve it at a later date. To perform an Update do the following:

1 From the Invoicing window select the invoices and credit notes for updating.

2 Click Update to display the Output options.

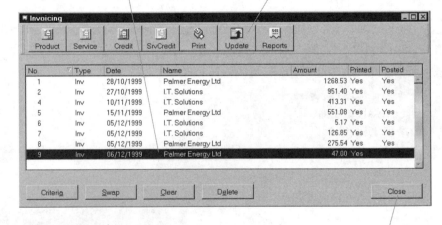

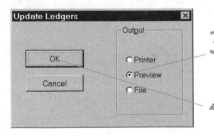

3 In the Output box click Preview.

4 Click OK to generate the update.

5 On the report, click Print to bring up the Windows Print dialog box, then click OK to print.

6 Click Close to return to the Invoicing window, then Close again.

Printing for Batch Invoicing

You can reprint your invoices as many times as you wish.

When you created Invoices or Credit Notes, both Product or Service, you may have decided to leave printing them until later as a batch. This can often save time when setting up file layouts and having to change the printer stationery.

For example, you may have created two Service invoices which now need printing. You would do the following:

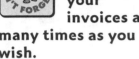

Use the Criteria button if you wish to print a number of invoices or credit notes that match a particular condition.

1 From the Invoicing window, select the invoices and credit notes for printing.

2 Click on the Print icon.

Select the correct layout file for printing your invoice or credit notes, depending upon which type of printer and paper size you are using.

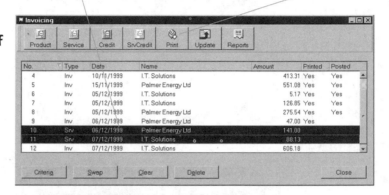

3 Ensure Preview is checked.

4 Select Layout required.

5 Click Run.

Standard layouts can be edited or new layouts created where necessary.

7 On the preview, click Print to bring up the Windows Print dialog box, then click OK to print.

6 Click Yes to confirm layout.

8 Click Close to return to the Invoicing window.

Producing Reports

The Reports option allows you to produce a wide range of reports about your product and service invoices, as well as your credit notes. Use these reports regularly to keep your business up to date. To print an invoice report:

Save time. Instead of searching through all your invoices for those not yet posted, use the Invoices Not Posted report.

1 Click Reports from the Invoicing toolbar.

2 Select report required.

3 Ensure Preview is selected.

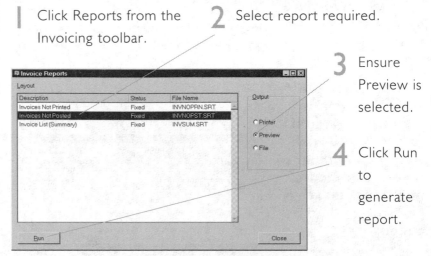

4 Click Run to generate report.

Use the Invoices Not Printed report regularly to keep up to date with sending out Invoices.

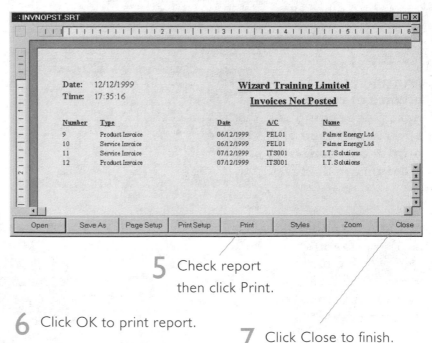

Alternatively, use the Criteria button on the Invoicing window to only list invoices not yet printed, posted, product only or service only etc.

5 Check report then click Print.

6 Click OK to print report.

7 Click Close to finish.

Financials

This Chapter shows you how to generate a variety of Financial reports so you can analyse your business transactions. This includes the Trial Balance, Profit and Loss, the Balance Sheet, the Budget and Prior Year reports. You will learn how to produce an automated VAT Return as well as a detailed Audit Trail, which lists every transaction recorded within the system.

Covers

Chapter Nine

The Financials Toolbar

From this toolbar you can generate all the financial reports you need to not only keep track of how your business is doing financially but also trace back and find out when certain transactions took place. The Audit Trail is particularly useful as it is a complete record of your transaction activities, whilst the VAT function gives you all the features you need to produce accurate VAT Returns.

To Produce the Audit Trail.

Run the Trial Balance Report.

To Produce the Profit and Loss Report.

To Produce the Balance Sheet Report.

To Produce the Budget Report.

Run the Prior Year Report.

To Produce a VAT Return.

The Audit Trail

Deleted transactions always appear in red.

The Audit Trail records details about transactions entered into the system and is a very useful source of information for checking and cross reference purposes. It may also be referred to when auditing your accounts.

Transaction codes used in the Audit Trail are explained on Page 59.

Sage Instant Accounting gives you a range of Audit Trail formats providing brief, summary or fully detailed reports which can be previewed, printed or saved as a file for use later. A report of deleted transactions can also be printed. Use the Audit Trail regularly to ensure your transactions are being recorded accurately. To view the Audit Trail:

Instant Accounting is capable of storing approximately 2,000,000,000 transactions in the Audit Trail (provided your computer has sufficient memory and disk space), so there may be no need to clear it.

1 From the Sage Instant Accounting toolbar, click Financials to bring up the Financials window displaying the Audit Trail.

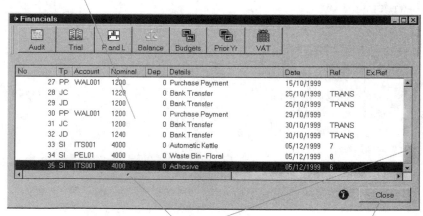

When you clear transactions from the Audit Trail, Sage Instant Accounting brings them forward as opening balances in your financial reports.

2 Use both horizontal and vertical arrow buttons and scroll bars to examine all transaction details.

3 When you have finished examining the Audit Trail, click Close.

To print the Audit Trail report

The Criteria box options vary according to the type of Audit Trail report selected.

All reports other than Brief will print in Landscape by default.

You can choose to exclude deleted transactions from your reports and instead, print them as a separate report later.

Print your Audit Trail reports at least every month for reference purposes.

1 From the Financials toolbar click Audit.

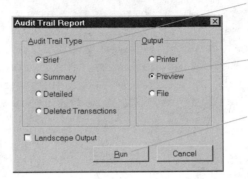

2 Select Audit Trail Type required, i.e. Brief.

3 Check Output is set to Preview.

4 Click Run to continue.

5 Enter required Criteria.

6 Click here to Exclude Deleted Transactions from the report.

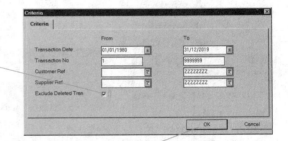

7 Click OK to continue.

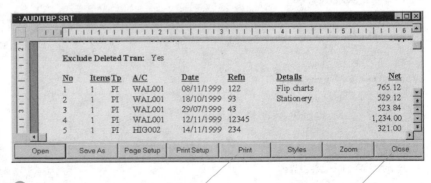

8 If you want to print the report, click Print, then OK.

9 Close the window.

The Trial Balance

You can run this report for any month. It proves a valuable source for management information.

This report displays a simple listing of current balances in all your nominal ledger accounts. It shows total values for both the debit and credit entries for all the nominal codes containing a balance value.

Because Instant Accounting controls the double-entry accounting for you, the debit and credit columns will always balance. To produce the Trial Balance report:

| From the Financials toolbar click Trial. This brings up the Criteria box.

Use the Zoom feature to help you preview the report more accurately before printing.

2 Ensure Preview is selected.

3 Click here and select period required. Scroll down if necessary.

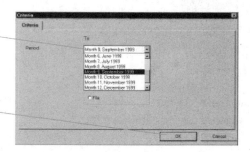

4 Click OK to generate the Trial Balance.

When you open the Financials window, the display automatically jumps down to the bottom of the list so the most recently entered transactions are displayed.

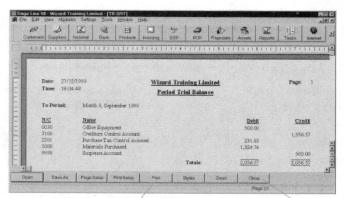

5 To print, click Print, then OK.

6 Click Close.

Profit and Loss Report

This important financial report details whether your business is trading at a profit over a particular period of time. The report can be produced for the current month or a range of consecutive months within your current financial year.

The balances of each of your income and expenditure nominal ledger accounts appear on the standard Profit and Loss report. These categories, i.e. Sales, Purchases, Direct Expenses and Overheads are grouped together and display a sub-total. The Gross Profit/(Loss) and Net Profit/(Loss) amount is also shown.

Balances are posted before the start of the financial year and so will appear as a prior year adjustment on the balance sheet, not on the Profit and Loss Report.

Unless you have set up your own layout, ensure you choose the Default Layout of Accounts in Step 3, otherwise you will not generate the correct report.

1 From the Financials window click P and L to bring up the Criteria box.

2 Enter the From and To Period required.

3 Select Default Layout of Accounts (1).

4 Ensure Preview is selected.

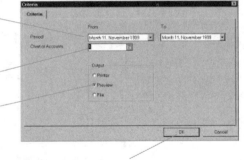

5 Click OK to generate P and L report.

You can set up your own Profit and Loss report layouts using the Chart of Accounts option from the Nominal Ledger toolbar.

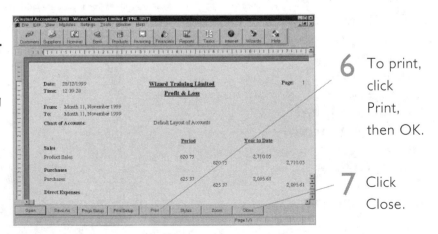

6 To print, click Print, then OK.

7 Click Close.

The Balance Sheet

Use the Balance Sheet regularly to give a summary of your current financial position.

The Balance Sheet details the financial position of a business at a particular moment in time by outlining its assets (what the business owns) and its liabilities (what the business owes). There are two main types of assets, fixed and current. Fixed assets are long-term and have material substance and include, for example, premises, equipment and vehicles, whilst current assets are continually changing and include stock, debtors, cash accounts etc.

The Balance Sheet shows the fixed and current assets, as well as the liabilities. By adding together the assets and subtracting the liabilities, the Balance Sheet shows the Capital, or net assets.

The difference between assets and liabilities is referred to as the company's net assets (or net worth).

1   Click Balance from the Financials toolbar to display the Criteria box.

2   Enter the From and To Period required.

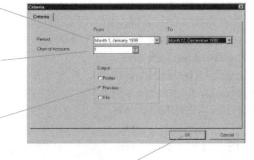

3   Select Default Layout of Accounts (1).

Liabilities consist of both current and long-term. Current liabilities are amounts owing at the balance sheet date and due for repayment within 12 months or less, e.g. trade creditors. Long-term liabilities are amounts due for repayment in more than 12 months, e.g. bank loan.

4   Ensure Preview is selected.

5   Click OK to generate Balance Sheet.

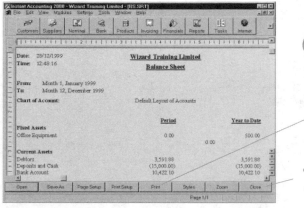

6   To print the Balance Sheet, click Print, then OK.

7   Click Close.

The Budget Report

You can amend your nominal account Budget values at any time by using the Global Changes feature from the Tools menu.

The Budget Report displays the current values in your purchases, sales, direct expenses and overhead account codes for the months you select and the year-to-date. Use this report to see how your business actually traded compared with the monthly budget you set against the nominal ledger accounts for the chosen months and the year to date.

1 Click Budgets from the Financials toolbar.

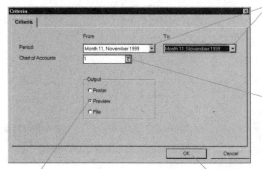

2 In the Criteria box enter the From and To Period required.

3 Select Default Layout of Accounts (1).

When you run a year end, Sage Instant Accounting offers you the option to move the actual monthly values for the year just ended to the budgets for the coming year. This sets the budget values to be what really happened in each month of the year just ended. You can also add a percentage increase to your budget values to reflect any anticipated rise in sales, purchases, costs, etc. for the coming year.

4 Ensure Preview is selected.

5 Click OK to generate the report.

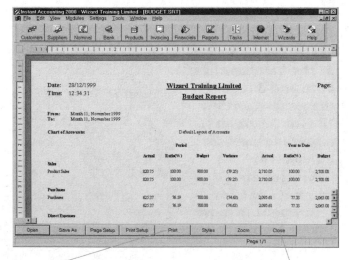

6 To print, click Print, then OK.

7 Click Close.

The Prior Year Report

The Prior Year report compares the current values in your purchases, sales, direct expenses and overhead accounts codes using the formats as set up for you in your chart of accounts. Trading activities are detailed for both the current month and the year-to-date, or alternatively for any period you specify.

Use the Prior Year report to compare your current trading results against how you did for the same period last year.

This report compares how your business is trading for the specified period against the same period in the previous year. Year-to-date totals and ratios are also included. To produce a Prior Year report, from the Financials window do the following:

1 Click Prior Yr to bring up the Criteria box.

2 Select Period required here.

3 Select Default Layout of Accounts (1).

To make a Prior Year Adjustment for your business refer to the Sage Instant Accounting Help Library Topics and search for Prior Year.

4 Check Output is set to Preview.

5 Click OK to continue.

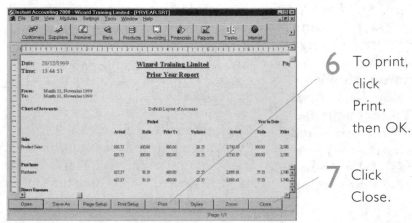

6 To print, click Print, then OK.

7 Click Close.

The VAT Return

Use the Wizard button to guide you through the VAT Return process.

Before reconciling your VAT transactions, you should back up your data files. Reconciling your transactions sets a flag against each transaction so it is automatically excluded from subsequent VAT Returns.

The Audit Trail VAT column shows whether a transaction is reconciled or not. R = reconciled; N = unreconciled; a hyphen (-) or a dash (–) = a non-VAT transaction.

For businesses that need to submit VAT Return forms to HM Customs and Excise, Sage Instant Accounting provides all the features to enable you to do this quickly and accurately, calculating both input and output tax for you from the information you have entered over the period. This is a prime reason for keeping accurate accounts.

Input tax is the VAT you are charged on your business purchases and expenses. Output tax is the VAT your business charges on it's taxable supplies or services. Because Value Added Tax is a tax charged to the final consumer, a business needs to calculate what input tax can be reclaimed and how much output tax needs paying to Customs and Excise. This is the purpose of the VAT Return.

You have the facility to set up 99 tax codes, but on installation Instant Accounting sets the standard UK and EC VAT rates for you, so you will probably not have to change anything. The default is set to the standard rate T1, presently at 17.5%, whilst others you may need are T0 (zero-rated) and T9 (transactions not involving VAT).

Within the nominal ledger are three accounts, namely the Sales Tax Control account (2200), Purchase Tax Control account (2201) and VAT liability account (2202). An accumulated total appears in the Sales account for the output tax charged to your customers whilst another accumulated total appears in the Purchase account for the input tax charged to your business.

When your VAT Return is due, enter the correct date range into the system and the program will calculate the difference between the input and output tax and will inform you of the net VAT due to either the Customs and Excise or yourselves.

After reconciling your VAT Return, VAT on the Sales and Purchases Control accounts for this VAT period need transferring to the VAT Liability nominal account. When a bank payment to the Customs and Excise is made or received, the VAT Liability account is cleared, leaving a zero balance.

Ensure all transactions have been reconciled and the **Audit Trail checked before running your VAT Return.**

Use the Wizard button to guide you through the VAT Return process.

Use the Calculate button to auto-matically calculate the totals for your VAT Return.

Three reports are available for printing: **Detailed, Summary and the VAT Return. The Detailed and Summary reports give a breakdown of all the totals from each box on the VAT Return.**

To produce your VAT Return

1 From the Financials window click VAT to bring up the VAT Return window displaying zero totals.

2 Enter the inclusive VAT period dates here.

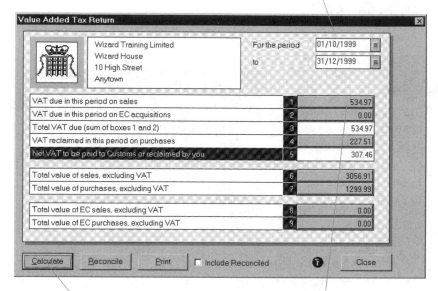

3 Click Calculate to calculate totals for this return. You will be informed if any unreconciled transactions have been found.

4 Click on a VAT total for a breakdown.

5 Double-click on T/C for a transaction breakdown.

6 Close each window to return to VAT Return.

7 Click Print, Run and OK to print the return.

Check that the balance of your VAT Return agrees with the balance of your VAT Control Accounts.

Use the VAT Transfer Wizard to transfer money from the Sales and Purchase Tax Control accounts to the VAT Liability account.

Sage Instant Accounting already has the following tax rates set up:

T0 = zero rated transactions.

T1 = standard rate.

T4 = sales to customers in EC.

T7 = zero rated purchases from suppliers in EC.

T8 = standard rated purchases from suppliers in EC.

T9 = transactions not involving VAT.

The VAT Transfer Wizard

Use the VAT Transfer Wizard to guide you through the transfer of your VAT liability once you have successfully reconciled and printed your VAT return.

1 From the Instant Accounting toolbar select Wizards, then click VAT Transfer Wizard.

2 Click Yes to confirm you wish to continue.

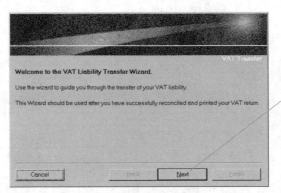

3 Click Next to proceed with the Wizard.

4 Work your way through each screen entering details where required and clicking Next until you reach the Confirm Posting Details window.

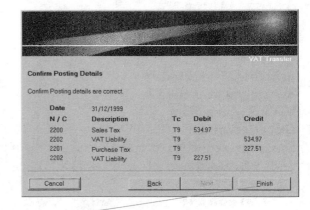

5 Click Finish to confirm details or Cancel to abandon.

Checking Your VAT Return

Before you actually print the VAT Return, you should always check that the figures are correct. The method for doing this varies depending on the VAT scheme you are using.

Refer to Chapter Five, Page 68 for instructions on printing Nominal Reports.

To check your VAT Return using the Standard VAT scheme

If you are using the Standard VAT scheme, the balance of your VAT Return and the balance of your VAT Control Accounts should agree. Check this as follows:

1 Click Print on the VAT Return (see Page 121) to bring up the VAT Return Report dialog box.

By default, the VAT on Sales control account is 2200 and the VAT on Purchases control account is 2201.

2 Select Detailed and Printer.

3 Click Run to print your Detailed VAT report.

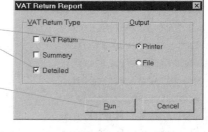

4 From the Instant Accounting toolbar, click Nominal, then Reports.

6 Check that the net closing balance of your VAT on Sales and VAT on Purchases control accounts agrees with the balance in box 5 of your VAT Return.

5 Print the Nominal Activity Report, using the control codes of your VAT on Sales and Purchases accounts and the date range of your VAT return.

If the figures still do not agree, the following reports could help you find the discrepancy:

• Audit Trail.

• Customers Day Book.

• Suppliers Day Book.

• Day Books for Bank, Cash and Credit Receipts and Payments.

If the figures do not agree, check that the VAT control account totals do not include a value for a tax code not included on your VAT Return, e.g. by default T9 is not included. Also check that you have not posted a transaction with the wrong date, or if you asked Instant Accounting to include any transactions it found outside the date range but not yet included in a VAT return.

Always ensure the VAT information for each transaction you enter in Sage Instant Accounting is correct to avoid wasting time later looking for errors.

To check your VAT Return using VAT Cash Accounting

If you are using the VAT Cash Accounting scheme, the balance of your VAT Return will not agree with the balance of your VAT control accounts, so you need to check your VAT Return as follows:

1 Click Print on the VAT Return (see Page 121) to bring up the VAT Return Report dialog box.

2 Select Detailed and Printer.

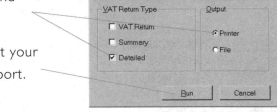

3 Click Run to print your Detailed VAT report.

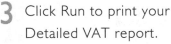

In the **Audit Trail VAT column, items marked with an N are included when you calculate your VAT Return. Items marked with an R have already been included on previous VAT Returns and have been reconciled for VAT and so are not included in this VAT Return.**

4 Refer to Page 114 and print the Audit Trail.

5 Using the same date range as your VAT Return, print the Day Books: Nominal Ledger report as detailed in Chapter Five, Page 68.

6 Again using the same date range as your VAT Return, from the Bank Reports window (Chapter Six, Page 84) print your Customer Receipts and Supplier Payments report.

7 From the Bank Reports window also print all your payment and receipt day book reports, using the same date range as Step 6.

 Make sure you have checked your VAT totals before printing your VAT Return.

8 Using all of the above reports, check that the totals on your VAT Return are correct.

Reconciling Your VAT Transactions

Instant Accounting does not auto- matically reconcile your transactions for you. You need to manually reconcile your transactions for VAT after you have calculated your VAT Return.

Once a transaction has been included on a VAT Return, it should be reconciled. This effectively marks the transaction as having been processed for VAT and by default it will therefore be excluded by Instant Accounting from subsequent VAT Returns.

The Audit Trail VAT column shows whether a transaction has been reconciled or not. N means it is unreconciled, R means it is reconciled and a dash or hyphen signifies that it is either a non-VAT transaction or that it has a VAT code that you have indicated should not be included in calculating the VAT Return. To reconcile your VAT transactions, do the following:

You should always back up your data files before reconciling your VAT transactions.

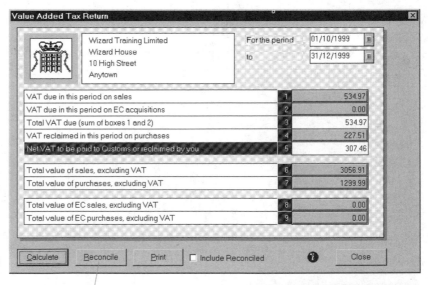

If a VAT transaction does not appear in your VAT Return when it should, check that you have not accidentally allocated it the default non-VAT transaction tax code T9.

1   Click Reconcile on the Value Added Tax Return.

2   Select Yes to confirm or No to abandon the action.

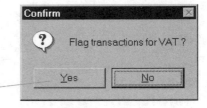

You can check that Sage Instant Accounting has flagged the transactions as reconciled by looking at the VAT column in the Audit Trail.

Clearing Your VAT Control Accounts

Only clear your VAT Control Accounts after fully reconciling and printing your VAT Return.

When you have prepared and checked your VAT Return and reconciled it, you should then transfer the values from your VAT on Sales and VAT on Purchases control accounts for the VAT period to your VAT Liability nominal account. This will make it easier for you later should you find a mistake and need to check through these accounts.

You clear the value you transfer to the VAT Liability account either when you subsequently make a VAT payment to HM Customs and Excise or, if VAT is owed to you, when you receive a refund from them.

You should clear your VAT control account only after fully reconciling and printing your VAT Return. Sage Instant Accounting provides the VAT Transfer Wizard to help you do this.

You can also start the VAT Transfer Wizard by clicking on the Wizards button on the Sage Instant Accounting toolbar and selecting VAT Transfer Wizard.

The procedure for clearing your VAT control accounts is different, depending on whether you are using the Standard VAT Scheme or VAT Cash Accounting. To run the VAT Transfer Wizard, do the following:

1 Click Modules from the Sage Instant Accounting menu bar and select the Wizards option.

2 Click on VAT Transfer Wizard.

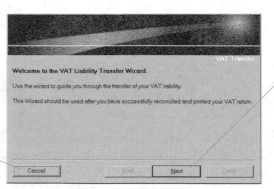

If you make a mistake, you can abort the VAT Transfer Wizard at any time by clicking on the Cancel button.

3 After confirming you wish to proceed, the VAT Transfer Wizard runs. See Page 122 and follow Steps 3–5.

Although you only have to fill in your VAT Return quarterly, we recommend that you follow the procedure monthly, simply because it is easier to reconcile one month's worth of transactions than three.

To clear your VAT Control Accounts using the Standard VAT Scheme

Open the Nominal Ledger window and make a note of the values of your VAT on Sales (2200) and VAT on Purchases (2201) control accounts. Also note whether each one is a debit or a credit, for example:

Nominal Ledger

N/C	Name	Debit	Credit
2200	VAT on Sales		7500
2201	VAT on Purchases	2500	

Once the relevant details have been noted, a Journal Entry needs posting from the Nominal Ledger transferring the values to the VAT Liability Account (2202). Using the details from the above example, the entry would be as follows:

Journal Entry

If you make a mistake, click on the Abandon button to clear your entries and start again.

N/C	Name	TC	Debit	Credit
2200	VAT on Sales	T9	7500	
2202	VAT Liability Account	T9		7500
2201	VAT on Purchases	T9		2500
2202	VAT Liability Account	T9	2500	

Once you have noted what entries you need to make, you can add them to the journal. When you process your journal by choosing Save, the VAT control accounts will be cleared.

You can only Save your journal entry when the value in the Balance box is zero.

To make the journal entries using the information you noted down as above, refer to Chapter Five, Page 61 and follow Steps 1–9.

By default, Sage Instant Accounting sets up the following VAT Control Accounts for you:

2200 – VAT on Sales

2201 – VAT on Purchases

2202 – VAT Liability Account

To clear your VAT Control Accounts using VAT Cash Accounting

If you use VAT Cash Accounting, first make a note of the values in box 1 (VAT due on sales) and box 4 (VAT reclaimed on purchases) on your Sage Instant Accounting VAT Return. Also note whether each is a positive or a negative value.

Let us assume, for example, that box 1 shows a positive value of 7500 and box 4 shows a positive value of 2500.

Using these details, a Journal Entry needs posting from the Nominal Ledger transferring the values to the VAT Liability Account (2202). From the above example, the entry would be as follows:

Journal Entry

N/C	Name	TC	Debit	Credit
2200	VAT on Sales	T9	7500	
2202	VAT Liability Account	T9		7500
2201	VAT on Purchases	T9		2500
2202	VAT Liability Account	T9	2500	

Unlike the Standard VAT Scheme, with VAT Cash Accounting the Sales and Purchase Tax Control Accounts rarely return to zero after you transfer the values shown on your VAT Return to the VAT Liability Account.

Once you have noted what entries you need to make, you can add them to the journal. When you process your journal by choosing Save, the VAT control accounts will be adjusted accordingly. You should note, however, that because of the way that VAT Cash Accounting works, the Sales and Purchase Tax control accounts very rarely clear to zero when you complete the above journal transfers.

To make the journal entries using the information you noted down as above, refer to Chapter Five, Page 61 and follow Steps 1–7.

The Report Designer

This chapter shows you how to create a new report and also how to edit an existing report to meet your own requirements. The Report Designer is very powerful and provides options for grouping and sorting information, adding calculations such as totals, setting up criteria and filters to search for information as well as designing the layout and format of the report.

Covers

Chapter Ten

Introducing the Report Designer

For more details about the Report Designer, click Reports from the Sage Instant Accounting toolbar and press F1.

When you first install Sage Instant Accounting, you can immediately generate and print all of the reports and stationery to suit most business needs. If you use stationery supplied by Sage, the data should fit in the pre-printed stationery forms without adjustment.

There will be occasions though when you need a new report not already supplied, or you need to modify an existing one to suit your specific needs. The Report Designer lets you do all of this to meet any specific requirements that you have.

The Report Designer, although an integral part of Instant Accounting, is actually a complete windows application on its own. The Designer has its own Title Bar, Menu Bar, and Desktop area on which you can open multiple document windows. Each document window can hold an entirely separate layout file, which means you can work on several layouts at once, if you wish. To run Report Designer:

You may need to click on the right scroll button on the Sage Instant Accounting toolbar to bring the Report button into view, depending on the screen area setting for your computer.

1 Select the Reports button from the Instant Accounting toolbar.

2 The Report Designer window appears.

3 Click here on each folder to see a list of existing layouts.

Use Report Designer to design new (or modify existing) reports to fit into any new pre-printed stationery forms your business may adopt.

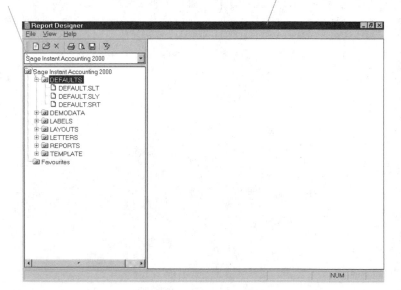

Running Existing Reports

Each of the main ledger windows, i.e., Customers, Suppliers, Nominal etc., gives you the option of printing existing reports related to that ledger. The appropriate chapters in this book have already shown you how to print these reports, but here is some additional information about generating reports that you need to be familiar with:

 Add report layouts which you use regularly to the Favorites folder on the Report Designer folders list. You can then easily locate those layouts in the future.

• If the report you selected has criteria enabled, a Criteria box will appear when you click on the Run button. Enter your criteria and click on OK to continue. If you do not change the default criteria values, all appropriate data will be included in your report.

• When you select to preview the report, the Preview window appears displaying the report. Once you have checked the report, you can send it for printing by clicking on the Print button.

• When you choose to print a report, a Print dialog box appears offering you a number of options. Use this box to specify which pages you want to print, how many copies you require, if they need collating or, if necessary, to change your printer settings.

 Any type of report layout can be placed in the Favorites folder – they do not all have to be of the same type.

• If you choose to print your report to a file, the Save File As dialog box appears. You need to enter a name for your file in the File Name box and to choose a folder and disk drive in which to store the file.

• You can create a number of different types of files, so that your report can be imported into other applications. The Save File as Type drop-down list box lets you select either Text File format (.TXT), Comma Separated Value (.CSV) or Report Data Files format (.SRD). When you have completed your selections, click on the OK button to save the report as a file.

Creating a new Report

The following example shows you how to create a Customer Balance and Credit List for a single customer or a range of customers using the Report Wizard. The report contains the Customer's account reference, company name and account balance, together with their credit limit. The report is sorted to show the customer with the lowest balance first. The report also displays a balance total.

When the Wizard is finished, the Report Designer appears with the new report/layout open ready for you to work on or preview.

1 From the Instant Accounting toolbar select Reports.

2 Click File and New from the Report Designer menu.

3 Select Customer option.

4 Click Next to continue.

5 Enter report Title here.

6 Click Next.

When your new report is complete, you can either save, preview, or print it.

7 The next screen confirms your selection. Click Next to progress to selecting report variables.

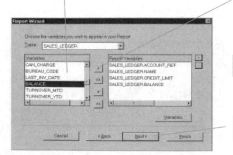

You can also double-click the required variable to copy it to the Report Variables view.

8 Select variable required from this list.

9 Click single right arrow button to copy to Report Variables view.

10 Repeat Step 9 for all required variables.

11 Click Next.

...cont'd

To make a selective choice of variables, hold down the CTRL key whilst clicking on variables required. Click the > button to transfer them as a group.

To highlight a range of variables, hold down the SHIFT key and click the first and last variable in the list. Select the > button to transfer the range as a group.

Should you ever need to transfer all the available variables simply click the >> button.

12 Grouping is not required, so just click Next.

13 Select SALES_ LEDGER.BALANCE.

14 Click > button.

15 Click Next.

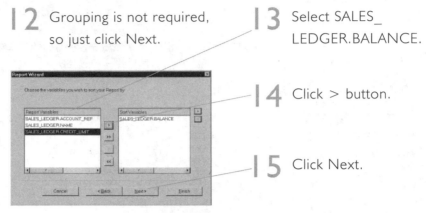

16 Select and move SALES_LEDGER .CREDIT_LIMIT from Total Variables to Report Variables.

17 Click Finish to generate the report layout.

The Report Designer now generates the appropriate report layout for you. You will be able to see how the layout is divided into sections, i.e., Page Header, Details, Page Footer, etc., and how the report variables have been arranged.

You will also notice that the report name and description has been automatically included for you in the page header by Sage Instant Accounting, together with the date and time for reference.

If the layout is not as required, you can modify the report later to suit your exact preferences. First, however, you need to check that it provides the information you require by running a report preview.

Previewing your Report

A report layout will look like this. To preview your report:

 Maximise your report layout window to view all the variables.

 Your report will appear in your Customers Reports window after saving.

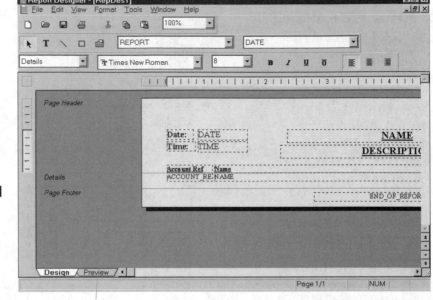

| Click Preview to run your new report.

2 If a Criteria box appears, carry out Steps 3–4, else go to Step 5.

3 Enter Criteria details.

 Be careful not to overwrite any existing reports. They may be useful to you later.

4 Click OK to run the report.

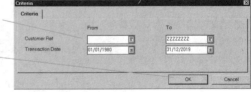

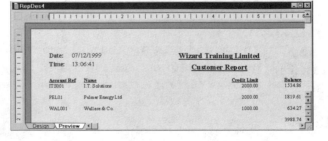

6 To close, click on File and Exit.

5 To save, select Save As from File menu, enter a filename and click OK.

Modifying your Report

To remove your company's name and address from all your layout files, select Company Preferences from the Settings menu on the Sage Instant Accounting toolbar. De-select the option by clicking the Print Name and Address on Stationery check box and click OK.

The Report Designer lets you modify your report layout, should you decide that changes are needed. The changed report can be saved under a new or the existing filename.

For example, you can modify the report just created and saved to sort customers into balance and credit limit order. As created, your report currently displays them only in balance order. This will make it easier to read for comparison purposes. Assuming your report is saved:

1 From the Customer toolbar click on the Reports option.

2 Select your report from the list and click Edit.

You can edit some Fixed Reports and save them to new filenames. The Original report remains unchanged and your new report is added to the list.

3 Click Format, Sorts.

4 In the Sorts box click Add.

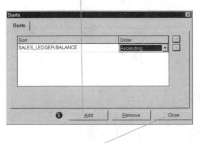

If you make a mistake designing the report, select immediately the Edit Undo option from the Edit menu.

7 Click Close, Preview and Save.

5 Select SALES_LEDGER .CREDIT_LIMIT.

6 Click OK.

Modifying an existing Report

You only have the chance to Edit Undo your last action. Therefore, check all of your work so that mistakes can be spotted immediately.

The Report Designer also lets you modify existing report layout files and some of the default reports supplied with the program. These should, however, be saved under a new filename.

For example, you can modify the supplied Customer List report to make it easier to read by increasing the details font size from the default 8 point to 10 point. At the same time you can make the Contact Name appear in bold. To make these changes, do the following:

1 From the Customer toolbar click on the Reports option.

2 Select the report from the list.

To see all of your variables in the report design, maximise the Report Designer window and use the vertical and horizontal scroll bar buttons as appropriate.

3 Click Edit to display the report layout.

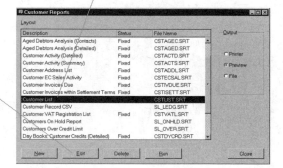

4 Double-click on CONTACT_NAME in the Details section to bring up the Object Properties box.

Switch between design and preview using these two tabs to help you quickly see how your layout changes will look.

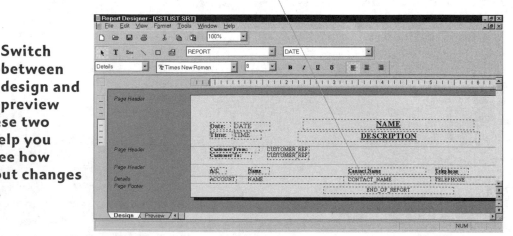

...cont'd

Do not be tempted to take a shortcut by using the buttons on the text toolbar when making these selective changes to the details, otherwise you may initiate changes in other parts of the report where they are not required.

5 Select the Font tab.

6 Click on Bold here to change the Font Style.

7 Click on 10 in the Size box to increase the size of the text.

Any text attributes you apply as described here override any text attributes applied through a text Style.

8 Click OK to implement the changes.

9 Now double-click on ACCOUNT_REF in the details section to bring up its Object Properties box and repeat Steps 7 and 8 only to increase the font size.

10 Repeat Step 9 for NAME, TELEPHONE and FAX respectively to also increase the font size of these three variables to 10 point.

You can also bring up the Object Properties box by clicking once on an item to select it, (e.g., ACCOUNT_REF) and simply pressing Enter on your keyboard.

11 Click on the Preview tab in the bottom left-hand corner of the Report Designer screen to view your modified report.

12 To save, select Save As from the Report Designer File menu, enter a suitable filename and click OK to save your changes as a new report.

Printing Report Information

Don't forget that help is always available by pressing the F1 key.

To save having to always go to the help menu to find out more information about a particular function within the Report Designer, you can take a printout of report information for keeping to hand. Make sure your printer is connected and powered up, then do the following:

1 Select Help, then Report Information... from the Report Designer menu bar.

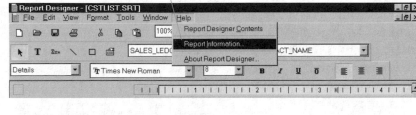

Sage Instant Accounting is set to print out all Report information by default.

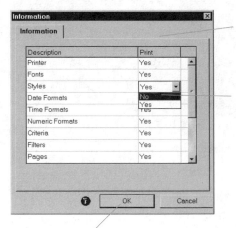

2 The Information window appears.

3 If there is any function you do not want to print out information for, e.g., Styles, Click here and select No.

When you have a query about reporting and printing, first look to see if the answer is included in the Common Questions and Answers section of the F1 help section.

4 Click OK to bring up the Print window.

5 Enter the number of copies you want here.

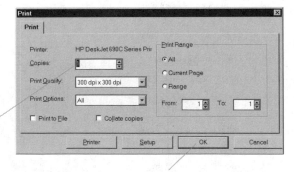

6 Click OK to print.

Opening Balances

This chapter explains how to enter opening balances for your customer, supplier, nominal accounts and your various bank accounts.

Covers

Chapter Eleven

Introduction

Print off a copy of the Opening Balances checklist from the F1 Help system to guide you.

It is important to set up opening balances correctly and in the right order. All accounts remain at zero until you enter opening balances for your Customers, Suppliers, Nominal and Bank.

Where opening balances are carried forward, accurate figures need entering to indicate the true financial position of the business, for example, its Debtors and Creditors and the Nominal Ledger Trial Balance.

Posted Opening Balances for your customers and suppliers are displayed in the trial balance report, which needs clearing before entering Opening Balances for the nominal ledger account, bank account and products.

Standard VAT and VAT Cash Accounting

Standard VAT calculates the VAT return on the invoices/ credits you have raised for your customers or received from your suppliers, and any bank/cash payments or receipts or journal entries with vatable tax codes.

Customer opening balances can be entered as lump sum balances. It is recommended, however, that each outstanding invoice and credit note be entered separately for cross referencing. Recording separate transactions will also provide accurate aged debtors analysis.

The second method, the VAT Cash Accounting scheme, is where the VAT return is calculated on the invoices/credits which you have received payment for from your customers or you have paid to your suppliers. Included too are any bank/cash payments or receipts or journal entries with vatable tax codes.

These are the Nominal Codes used in the Trial Balance:

1100 = Debtors Control Account

2100 = Creditors Control Account

9998 = Suspense Account.

With VAT Cash Accounting each invoice and credit note must be entered for your customers individually, with the correct tax code.

The same Standard VAT and VAT Cash Accounting conditions apply for entering opening balances for suppliers. Again it is recommended for Standard VAT that separate transactions be recorded for outstanding invoices and credit notes to match up with payments later instead of grouping them all together in one opening balance. Separate transactions will again provide accurate aged creditors information.

Opening Balances – Standard VAT

Follow the same procedures as for Customers when entering opening balances for your Suppliers.

With the Standard VAT accounting method, opening balances can be entered as a lump sum or individual transactions. You set up your customer balances using the Customer Record, accessed by using the Customers button on the Sage Instant Accounting toolbar.

Where customer information exists already, you can refer to the Aged Debtors Analysis and Detailed Customer Activity reports for cross referencing purposes and for checking that opening balances are recorded accurately. The Aged Creditors and Detailed Supplier Activity reports are also available for your suppliers.

When entering a total for outstanding invoices/credit notes, O/BAL is a useful reference.

To enter customer Opening Balance details

From the Customers window click on the required record, then click Record on the toolbar.

By recording the original invoice/credit note date, you will have accurate details of overdue debtors.

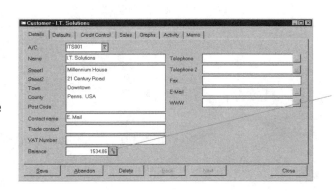

2 Click here to set up Opening Balance.

Use Next and Back buttons to move between customers.

3 Enter invoice/credit note number.

4 Enter original transaction date or last date of previous financial year.

5 Enter Type.

6 Enter Gross amount.

7 Click Save to record details or Cancel to abandon.

T9 is set as the default non-vatable tax code.

Opening Balances – VAT Cash Accounting

To enter Opening Balances for your suppliers, click on the Suppliers button, then follow the steps you would with Customers.

Using this particular scheme each customer invoice and credit note needs entering individually with the correct tax code because VAT is only considered when payment is being made. The opening balances can be entered via the Batch Invoices or Credits screens.

To enter customer Opening Balance details

1 From the Customers window click on the required record, then click Record on the toolbar.

Use Audit Trail from Financials to identify reference numbers.

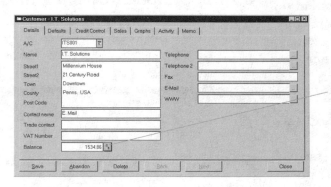

2 Click here to set up Opening Balance.

Enter original date of invoice or credit note for accurate aged debtors analysis or last date of previous financial year.

3 Enter invoice/credit note number.

4 Enter original transaction date or last date of previous financial year.

5 Enter Type.

The default tax code and VAT appear automatically, but can be changed if necessary.

6 Enter Net amount. If you want to enter a single opening balance for this customer, enter total net amount of all invoices here.

7 Tax Code and VAT are entered for you. Change if necessary then click Save to record details or Cancel to abandon.

Clearing Opening Balances from Trial Balance

Always print a copy of your Trial Balance report BEFORE clearing the opening balances.

When opening balances for your customers and suppliers are saved, they are posted to the trial balance. These entries need clearing or they will be duplicated when posting opening balances for your nominal ledger accounts. This will produce an incorrect balance sheet.

Before you start, make a note from your trial balance of the values of your Debtors and Creditors Control Accounts, your Sales Tax and Purchase Tax Control Accounts and your Suspense Account and whether each one is a debit or a credit, for example:

If you are using VAT Cash Accounting, balances need clearing in your Sales and Purchase Tax Control Accounts.

Trial Balance

N/C	Name	TC	Debit	Credit
1100	Debtors Control Account	T9	30,687.19	
2100	Creditors Control Account	T9		21,189.78
9998	Suspense Account	T9		9,497.41
	BALANCE		30,687.19	30,687.19

When entering journal entries into the transaction table, use opposite values from the trial balance, i.e., Debit (+) and Credit (-).

Once the relevant details have been noted, a Journal Entry from the Nominal Ledger needs to be made to clear the balances. Using the details from the above example, the entry would be as follows:

Journal Entry

N/C	Name	TC	Debit	Credit
1100	Debtors Control Account	T9		30,687.19
2100	Creditors Control Account	T9	21,189.78	
9998	Suspense Account	T9	9,497.41	
	BALANCE		30,687.19	30,687.19

The journal entry can only be saved when the value in the Balance box is zero.

...cont'd

Always bear in mind that for a journal entry, VAT is neither calculated for you nor posted to the VAT control account.

Once you have noted what entries you need to make, you can add them to the Journal. When you process these entries, the opening balances in the Trial Balance will be cleared. To make the entries do the following:

1 Click Nominal from the Instant Accounting toolbar.

3 The Ref. entry is optional. Type a reference if desired.

2 Click on Journals from the Nominal Ledger window to bring up the Journals window.

4 Check for correct Date.

Use the Finder button to quickly locate the correct codes.

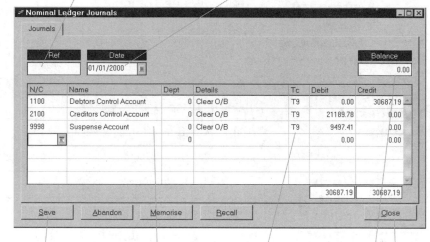

N/C	Name	Dept	Details	Tc	Debit	Credit
1100	Debtors Control Account	0	Clear O/B	T9	0.00	30687.19
2100	Creditors Control Account	0	Clear O/B	T9	21189.78	0.00
9998	Suspense Account	0	Clear O/B	T9	9497.41	0.00
		0			0.00	0.00

Ref / Date 01/01/2000 / Balance 0.00

Total: 30687.19 / 30687.19

Save | Abandon | Memorise | Recall | Close

If you make a mistake just click on the Abandon button and start again.

5 Enter details for both the credit and debits.

6 Note, the default Tax code of T9 is entered for you by Sage.

7 Check total Debit and Credit are equal and a zero balance is displayed in the Balance box.

8 Click Save to process your journal or Abandon to cancel.

9 Click Close to return to Nominal Ledger window.

Entering Balances Part Way through the Year

Sage Instant Accounting can only produce accurate reports if the information you enter is correct. This, therefore, is a good time to check that Customer and Supplier details are still up to date.

Sage Instant Accounting needs Opening Balances in order to produce accurate financial statements. Because all accounts in all the ledgers have a zero balance when the program is first installed, it is important that the Opening Balances are entered as soon as possible. Without them your financial statements will not be accurate.

It is, however, quite possible to start using Instant Accounting at any time through your financial year, and then enter the Opening Balances as and when they become available. For instance, if you have been in business for some time you will already have stock, products, customers and suppliers. You will have a transaction history. When you first start to use Sage Instant Accounting you will set up Records for your Customers, Suppliers, Products etc. This is when you can start to enter some Opening Balances.

If you do start to use Sage Instant Accounting part way through your financial year, you should contact your accountant as soon as possible for a detailed list showing all your outstanding Debtors and Creditors. You can then use this as the Opening Balances for your Customers and Suppliers.

Simply click on the button on each Supplier, Customer, Bank Account and Nominal Ledger record to enter the opening balance for that account.

You also need to ask for a Trial Balance from your accountant, which will give you the Opening Balances for each Nominal Ledger and Bank account.

You must at all times make sure that the information you enter is accurate. If you need to enter Opening Balances part way through your financial year, you will probably have a lot of Nominal Ledger opening balances to enter! It is important, therefore, that you enter these accurately otherwise your balance sheet will be incorrect.

You will also need to enter any year-to-date values from your Profit and Loss accounts. Your accountant should be able to provide you with this.

Nominal Ledger and Bank Account

If you have money in the bank or building society, their statement shows you have a balance under the credit column. They owe you that money, you are the creditor. When this money is recorded in your accounts, such asset balances are recorded the opposite way round as debits. If you have money in your bank or building society, the balance must be entered as a debit.

Before entering your Nominal Ledger opening balance, you must first clear the opening balances from your trial balance, as shown on Page 143.

When entering opening balances for your Nominal Ledger or Bank account, double-entry postings are applied by Sage Instant Accounting. For example, if you post a debit opening balance of £100 to your Building Society account (1220 by default), Instant Accounting automatically posts £100 as a credit to your Suspense Account (9998 by default).

After you have entered all your Nominal Ledger and Bank account opening balances, the balance of the Suspense Account should be zero again. A new trial balance needs printing to check opening balances have been included for all your nominal accounts. If you still have a balance in the Suspense Account (i.e. it is not zero), an opening balance may have been omitted or a debit or credit misposted.

Nominal ledger opening balances

1 From the Instant Accounting toolbar, select Nominal.

2 Click on the required account.

3 Click on the Record button.

4 Click the O/B button to enter the balance.

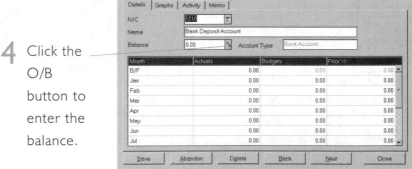

5 Enter opening balance details here.

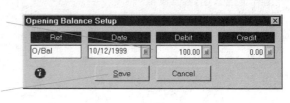

6 Click Save, then Close.

Bank Opening Balances

You can also set up a Bank account Opening Balance directly from the Bank Record. To do this follow these steps:

Enter an opening balance for each nominal account code that appears on your trial balance.

1 From the Sage Instant Accounting toolbar, select Bank.

2 Click on the Bank Record you wish to set up an Opening Balance for and click on Record.

You can enter Bank account opening balances either through the Bank Record or through the Nominal Ledger Record, but not both.

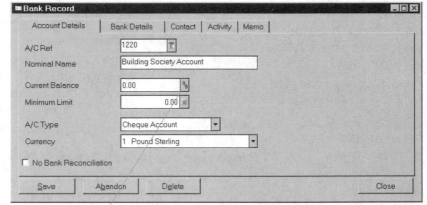

3 Click the O/B button to bring up the Opening Balance Setup box.

An asset should always have a debit entry, whilst a liability should always have a credit entry.

4 Enter Date if different from default date.

5 Enter opening balance as a Receipt or Payment. If you have money in your bank, this will be a Receipt.

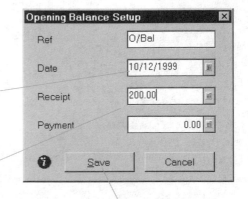

6 Click Save to record the Opening balance information.

Changing from VAT Cash to Standard VAT Accounting

Changing from VAT Cash Accounting to the Standard VAT Scheme should be carried out either at a VAT quarter end or at a month end, after the VAT on the Cash Accounting scheme has been reconciled and before any transactions are entered under the Standard VAT Scheme.

Small businesses often need to watch their cash flow, so the VAT Cash Accounting scheme was devised to help small companies whose expected annual taxable turnover does not exceed a certain amount.

This amount is specified by the Customs and Excise and many businesses use VAT Cash Accounting, especially in the early years of trading. However, once this taxable turnover value is exceeded, your company must change to Standard VAT Accounting.

On the VAT Cash Accounting scheme, you pay and reclaim VAT on actual payments received or issued, whereas on the Standard VAT Scheme you pay VAT on invoices or credit notes issued or received. Contact your local VAT office for more information about VAT schemes and to find out which scheme your company should be using.

Preparing to switch from VAT Cash Accounting to the Standard VAT Scheme

Before switching VAT schemes, do the following:

Contact your local VAT office to find out the current VAT Cash Accounting annual taxable turnover limit, and for all VAT related enquiries.

1 Backup your Instant Accounting data and clearly label it 'Before switching to Standard VAT Accounting'.

2 Produce your VAT Return, as shown on Page 121.

3 Print and reconcile your VAT return, as per Page 125.

4 Having reconciled your VAT Return, in the VAT Return window click on the Reconcile button to set the reconciliation flags on your transactions.

5 Post the journal entries to transfer the VAT from your Sales and Purchase Tax Control Accounts to your VAT Liability Account.

You are now ready to switch to Standard VAT Accounting.

...cont'd

When you change to Standard VAT Accounting, you will become liable for the VAT on the invoices you send to your customers or receive from your suppliers. This means that you will sometimes be paying VAT to the Customs and Excise on invoices that you have not received payment for yet. This is where the VAT Cash Accounting scheme benefits the smaller business and aids cash flow.

To switch from VAT Cash Accounting to the Standard VAT Accounting Scheme

Check that you have produced your VAT Return correctly, that all transactions have been reconciled and the necessary journal entries accurately posted, then do the following:

1 Click on Settings on the Instant Accounting menu bar.

2 Click on Company Preferences.

3 Choose the Parameters tab.

Settings
- Company Preferences...
- Customer Defaults...
- Supplier Defaults...
- Product Defaults...
- Invoice Defaults...
- Financial Year...
- Change Program Date...
- Tax Codes...
- Currency...
- Departments...
- Product Categories...
- Control Accounts...
- Finance Rates...
- Change Password...

Company Preferences

Address | Labels | Parameters

Printing
☐ Print End of Report Banner

VAT Defaults
☐ Item VAT Amendable   ☐ VAT Cash Accounting
Non-Vatable Tax Code   T9 0.00

Others
☐ Exclude deleted transactions   ☐ No Warning on Visa receipts
                                    ☐ No Recurring entries at startup
                                    ☐ Display Account Status
☐ List PP/SR by split   ☐ Group items in Bank Rec

OK | Cancel

4 Deselect the VAT Cash Accounting check box.

5 Click OK.

Always check your values carefully when working out VAT to avoid problems later.

6 To ensure the VAT reconciled earlier is not reclaimed again under the new scheme, produce and reconcile your VAT Return again, choosing to set the Reconciliation flags.

7 With Standard VAT Accounting, the VAT amount showing on the Sales and Purchase Tax control accounts becomes liable to Customs & Excise. If correct, post a journal entry to transfer the amounts to your VAT Liability Account.

Your system is now on Standard VAT Accounting.

Supplier Opening Balances

The procedure for entering supplier opening balances is very similar to that for entering customer opening balances. Refer to Page 141.

For your suppliers, you should only enter the opening balances once you have finished entering all of your customer, suppliers and nominal account details, including your bank accounts.

You can enter your supplier opening balances either as a lump sum, or you can enter each transaction separately. The latter is more tedious, but is useful if you need to later refer back to how the opening balance was made up. As with your customers, you post the opening balances for your suppliers using the O/B button on each supplier record.

The method you use for entering opening balances for your suppliers is different depending on whether you are on the VAT Cash Accounting or the Standard VAT Accounting Scheme.

T9 is set as the default non-vatable tax code.

For VAT Cash Accounting, you should enter each invoice and credit note for your suppliers individually, making sure that you use the correct tax code.

If you are using the Standard VAT Scheme, you have the choice of either entering your supplier opening balances as lump sum balances or you can enter each outstanding invoice and credit note separately. It is recommended that you enter your opening balances as separate transactions to make it easier for you to match payments later.

These are the Nominal Codes used in the Trial Balance:

1100 = Debtors Control Account

2100 = Creditors Control Account

9998 = Suspense Account.

Do not forget that when you have finished entering the opening balances for your suppliers and customers you need to clear the values from the Creditors and Debtors Control Accounts and your Suspense Accounts. If you fail to do this, these postings will be duplicated when you post the opening balances for your Nominal Ledger accounts and your Balance Sheet would be incorrect.

You can use the Trial Balance report to clear the Creditors and Debtors Control Accounts and your Suspense Account, as it shows the balances of the postings made when you saved the opening balances for your suppliers and customers. See Page 143 for clearing opening balances.

Data Management

This chapter shows you important routines and procedures you need to use regularly for taking care of your data. Often data entered into the system is lost or corrupted by not following simple file maintenance. Backing up of data is essential to any business as problems often occur at the most inconvenient and crucial times.

Covers

Chapter Twelve

Backing up Data

It is advisable to run the data check option before you back up your data.

Always keep your backups in a safe, secure place.

Use the Options button to select what to backup – all your files, just your reports and/or layout templates, or only your data files.

The files you are backing up must have the correct extension to be included in the backup.

Regular data backup (at least once daily) is essential in case of system error, when valuable data can be corrupted and sometimes lost. If this happens, you can at least restore important data files, reports and/or layout templates from your most up-to-date backup. A backup routine is provided by Sage Instant Accounting to automatically backup to your computer's Floppy Drive A:, but this can be changed to save to any drive and/or directory you require.

Backing up procedures vary from business to business, some use five disks for Monday to Friday and repeat their usage the following week. The important thing is to backup your data at least once a day! Sage Instant Accounting always prompts you to back up when you Exit the program, but to perform a backup at any other time do the following:

1 From the Sage Instant Accounting menu, click on File.

2 Click on Backup.

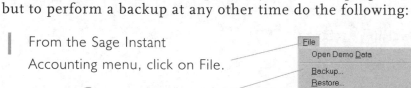

3 To backup to Instant Accounting's default Drive A, click OK; else, to save to another drive or directory, follow Steps 4–7.

4 To change backup destination, click Setup.

5 Select correct drive.

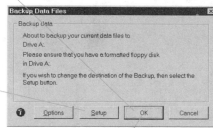

7 Click OK, then OK in the Backup Data Files dialog.

6 Select directory if appropriate.

Restoring Data

It is always advisable to run the Check Data option from File, Maintenance after you have restored your data.

Hopefully you should never have to restore your files, but should you be unlucky and suffer data loss or corruption, the Restore procedure allows you to revert to a previous backup. Which backup you restore from is up to you, but it will normally be the most recent.

The Restore facility allows data from your backup disks to replace your old data by erasing it and starting again. It is therefore very important to correctly label disks when you take a backup, and always keep them in a safe place. You may even consider keeping them somewhere other than on the premises in case of fire or theft!

Restoring data will erase the current Instant Accounting data and replace it with data from your backup disks.

Because the restore procedure erases your old data, any data you entered since the backup is lost and will need entering again. Make sure that the Restore is first necessary, then do the following:

1 From the Sage Instant Accounting menu, click on File.

2 Click on Restore.

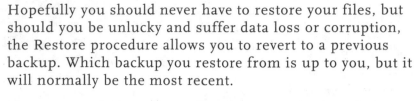

You must restore ALL your data, not just selective data files or a mismatch may exist between the ledger data, causing data corruption.

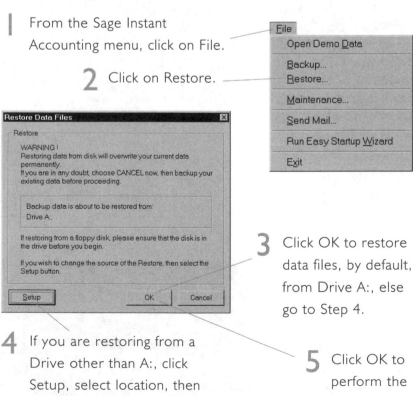

3 Click OK to restore data files, by default, from Drive A:, else go to Step 4.

4 If you are restoring from a Drive other than A:, click Setup, select location, then click OK to return to this box.

5 Click OK to perform the restore.

Changing Global Values

Certain values in Sage Instant Accounting, such as Credit Limits, have applications throughout the program. From time to time certain record values may need changing for all your records or for a selected group. To save time, these values can be changed quickly and easily by using the Global Changes Wizard. The Wizard guides you with on-screen instructions to make the necessary changes where required.

Values within the customer, supplier and nominal ledger records can be changed as well as certain values within your product records, for example the product sales price could be increased globally by 5% for a range of products. To run the Wizard:

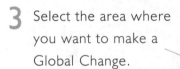

1 From the Sage Instant Accounting menu, select Tools.

2 Click on Global Changes to start the Wizard.

3 Select the area where you want to make a Global Change.

4 Click Next to continue.

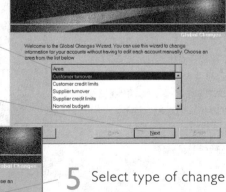

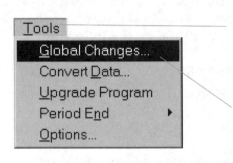

5 Select type of change required.

6 Click Next to continue.

...cont'd

To exit from a wizard at any point, choose the Cancel button or press ALT + F4.

Use the Global Changes Wizard to quickly set up Credit Limits for all your Customers and to record your credit limit from your Suppliers.

Always check you have entered the correct information as you may not be able to easily undo changes.

7 You must enter a value here before Sage Instant Accounting will let you progress.

8 Click Next to continue.

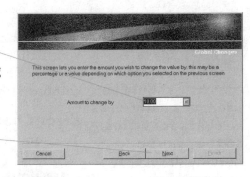

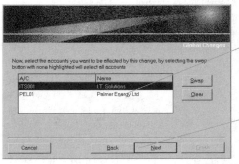

9 Select records required.

10 Click Next to continue.

11 Check that the details are correct. If you need to make any changes, use the Back button until you get to the appropriate screen, make the changes, then keep clicking Next to get back to this screen.

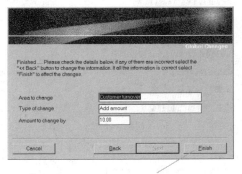

12 Click Finish to action the changes.

Whilst the Global Changes Wizard allows you to make changes quickly and easily, be very careful when using it and always double-check your values because when you click Finish, the changes you have entered are immediately actioned. In some cases these are quite major changes, such as increasing all product sales prices by a stated percentage. If you were to accidentally enter the wrong percentage, you cannot easily undo the resulting price changes!

File Maintenance

The Check Data option should be used on a daily basis to check for errors, so they can be quickly detected and rectified.

Sage Instant Accounting provides four important maintenance options to manage and check the validity of your data files. These features include checking for input errors, allowing manual data error corrections, data compression and building new data files.

Error Checking

You should use the Check Data facility to check the validity of your data files. If necessary you can then make corrections where required. This facility needs to be run regularly, before taking backups and after restoring data.

If there are problems whilst checking the data, a File Maintenance Problem Report dialog box appears which includes a Summary, Comments, Errors or Warnings.

1 From the Sage Instant Accounting menu, select File.

2 Click Maintenance.

3 From the File maintenance window click Check Data.

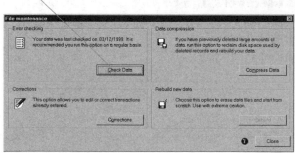

4 Checking Data Files box shows the progress.

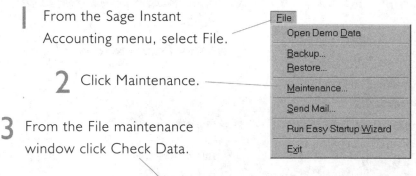

To print out an error report, select the category tab required from the File Maintenance Problems Report dialog box and click the Print button.

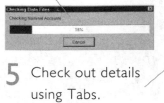

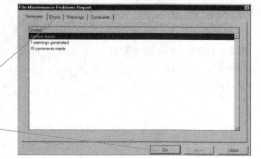

5 Check out details using Tabs.

6 Click Fix to correct errors, else Close.

For more information click on the 𝒾 button on the File Maintenance dialog box.

The File Maintenance Report

You can view any reported problems following a data check using the various tabs in the File Maintenance Problems Report dialog box. The Summary tab simply lists a summary of Sage Instant Accounting's findings during the data check. The findings themselves are broken down into three types of data inconsistency, as follows:

Errors	Errors flag serious data problems. However, most of these errors can often be corrected by Sage Instant Accounting when you select the Fix option.

Errors are serious data problems and should be rectified as soon as possible.

Warnings	Warnings are not as serious as Errors, but they do highlight problems that you should attend to promptly. You may not be able to correct warnings through the use of the Fix button, so they may require correcting manually.
Comments	Comments are the least serious of the data problems detected by Instant Accounting and do not require immediate attention. They do, however, highlight minor inconsistencies in the data, which you should at some stage correct.

Use the Fix button to instruct Instant Accounting to rectify your data error problems.

If Sage Instant Accounting does report errors, you should try to deal with them as soon as possible, but remember that it is advisable to make a backup before attempting any corrections – just in case!

Make sure you take a backup of your data before running any file maintenance routines or fixing errors etc.

Most data errors can be corrected by using the Fix option on the Maintenance Report. Instant Accounting first makes the corrections to a temporary copy of the relevant data file. Then, if the data correction is successful, the temporary file is used to replace the original file containing corrupted data.

If needed, you can print out an Error, Warnings or Comments report by clicking on the Print button in the File Maintenance Problems Report dialog box.

Error Corrections

 The reference field can be amended in the Edit Transaction Allocation Record.

 Use the Edit button to amend any reference for payments or receipts made against a transaction.

 Use the Find button to search for transactions.

Journal entries cannot be amended using the Edit button. To do so select the Journals option from the Nominal Ledger toolbar and make the necessary adjustment by posting a journal entry with the opposite values.

Correcting Transactions

Any mistakes made while entering transactions can be corrected using the Corrections option from the File Maintenance window. These transactions, however, can only be edited or deleted if they are still held in the Audit Trail. To correct a transaction:

1   Click Corrections from the File Maintenance window.

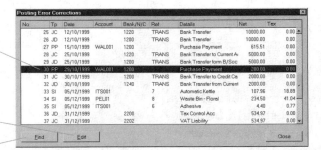

2   Select transaction to correct.

3   Click Edit.

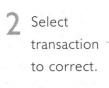

4   For changes to the customer/supplier account, bank, details, reference or date, make your corrections here.

5   For more changes click Edit.

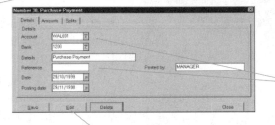

6   To change the nominal account, details, department, amount or VAT amount/code, make your corrections here.

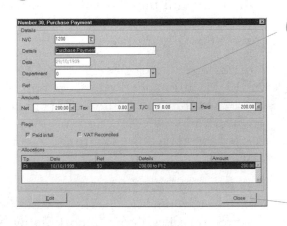

7   Close and Save.

The Reverse button only appears if the transaction has been reconciled on the VAT Return, otherwise the dialog box shows a Delete button.

Reversing VAT Reconciled Transactions

You can delete a transaction provided it has not been reconciled on the VAT Return. However, any VAT reconciled transaction will display a Reverse button instead of the Delete button in the Transaction Record window. To reverse VAT reconciliation on a transaction:

1 From the Posting Error Corrections window, select transaction and click Edit.

2 To reverse VAT reconciliation click on the Reverse button.

3 Click Yes to confirm.

After confirming a reversal of VAT reconciliation, the Ref entry in the Posting Errors Corrections box reads 'Cancel'.

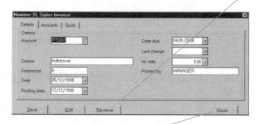

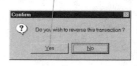

4 Close all windows.

Data Compression

When there has been a lot of activity, such as deletion or amendments of any records, use the Compress Data option to produce a new set of data files. Sage Instant Accounting will then reduce file size by removing these deleted records, freeing up disk space. To perform data compression, do this:

1 Click Compress Data from the File Maintenance box.

2 Click Compress.

Make sure you take a back up of your data files BEFORE running Compress Data as the action is irreversible.

3 Compress Data Files box shows the Progress.

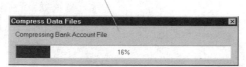

4 Click Close.

Rebuilding Data Files

Take care when using the Rebuild option as it will clear the contents of your existing data files. USE WITH CAUTION.

This Sage Instant Accounting option is for creating a new or just a selected set of data files. You may, for example, wish to practice entering transactions when you first install Sage Instant Accounting and before you start using it for real. You may even want to experiment with creating your own Chart of Accounts.

When you are ready to start using Instant Accounting for your business transactions, you will need to clear this practice data and create a fresh set of data files. To do this, from the File Maintenance window do the following:

If you have been familiarising yourself with Instant Accounting and entering trial data, use the Rebuild option to clear this dummy data and create a new set of data files for you.

1 Click on the Rebuild button to run the option.

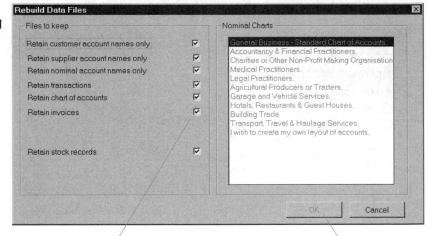

Rebuild Data Files

Files to keep

Retain customer account names only	☑
Retain supplier account names only	☑
Retain nominal account names only	☑
Retain transactions	☑
Retain chart of accounts	☑
Retain invoices	☑
Retain stock records	☑

Nominal Charts

General Business - Standard Chart of Accounts.
Accountancy & Financial Practitioners.
Charities or Other Non-Profit Making Organisation
Medical Practitioners.
Legal Practitioners.
Agricultural Producers or Traders.
Garage and Vehicle Services.
Hotels, Restaurants & Guest Houses.
Building Trade
Transport, Travel & Haulage Services.
I wish to create my own layout of accounts.

OK   Cancel

Instant Accounting always prompts you to confirm that you want to rebuild your data files. Make sure you really want to before clicking Yes.

2 Select the files to rebuild by removing the check here.

3 Click OK.

4 Click Yes here to confirm you want to rebuild your data files.

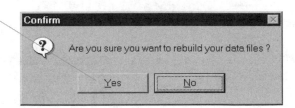

Confirm

? Are you sure you want to rebuild your data files ?

Yes   No

Period End

This chapter shows you how to carry out necessary routine functions at your month and year ends. You will also learn how to prepare Sage Instant Accounting so it is ready for you to start entering transactions for a new financial year.

Chapter Thirteen

Running Period End Functions

If program date needs changing for the Month End procedure, select Change Program Date from the Settings menu. Remember to re-set the date back to the correct date.

Period End options are essential monthly and year end procedures for updating the accounting system, for example, for posting accruals, prepayments and depreciation. The Audit Trail can then be cleared of any unwanted transactions.

Through running these procedures, you will also be preparing Sage Instant Accounting so that you are ready to enter transactions for the new financial year.

Month End

At each month end it is important to post your prepayments, accruals and depreciation values. Instant Accounting will process these transactions automatically and update your nominal account records and audit trail. The option also exists to clear down your month to date turnover figures for your customer and supplier records.

Always Backup your data files before and after Month End procedures.

Once you have run the Month End procedures, this is an opportune time to produce some of your financial reports, for example, the Profit and Loss, Balance Sheet, Trial Balance, Budget and Prior Year Analysis reports. Customer statements and Aged analysis reports for Debtors and Creditors will also prove useful.

Month End Guidelines

Here is a check list for the Month End:

Use File Maintenance Check and Compress Data options to check your files.

1   Check all relevant transactions have been posted.

2   Check recurring entries have been set up and processed.

3   Check prepayments, accruals and depreciation have been set up.

Refer to the Instant Accounting Library Help system for more information about running Month End procedures.

4   Complete your bank reconciliation.

5   Print Day Books for customers, suppliers, banks and nominal ledger, and ledger activity reports.

6   Post product journals for your profit and loss and balance sheet.

The month end routine is necessary if you have Recurring Entries, Prepayments, Accruals, Depreciation, or you wish to clear down the turnover figures for Customers and Suppliers.

The Year End is an ideal time to remove any fully paid transactions or unwanted records, leaving only outstanding items on your ledgers at the start of the new Financial Year.

Select the Clear Turnover Figures check box to set your month to date turnover figures to zero on each customer and supplier record screen.

After following the Month End guidelines it is time to run the month end procedure. You will probably want to run it on a day other than the actual last calendar day of the month, as this is often more convenient. You will, therefore, have to change the program date first. To do this, simply follow these steps:

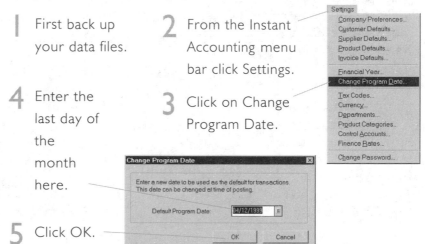

1 First back up your data files.

2 From the Instant Accounting menu bar click Settings.

3 Click on Change Program Date.

4 Enter the last day of the month here.

5 Click OK.

6 From the Instant Accounting menu, click on Tools.

7 Select Period End.

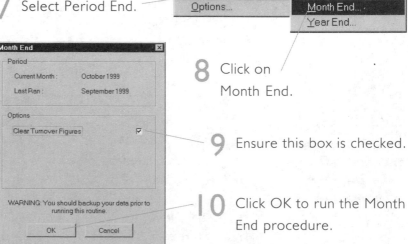

8 Click on Month End.

9 Ensure this box is checked.

10 Click OK to run the Month End procedure.

For additional information about running the Year End Procedure and Checklist refer to the Library Help system.

Take at least two backups of your data files before and after running the Year End routine.

Use File Main-tenance to check for errors, correct and compress data files and maximise disk space.

After Year End check your Financial Year Start Date is correct before entering new transactions.

Year End

Before you run the Year End, Month End procedures must first be completed, together with any final adjustments.

First, when you run Month End on the last month of the current financial year, DO NOT clear the Audit Trail. Once values for the month end have been checked and you are satisfied that they are correct, set the program date to the last date of the current financial year and run Year End:

1 Set the program date to the last day of the financial year by carrying out Steps 1–5 on Page 163.

2 From the Instant Accounting menu, click on Tools.

3 Select Period End.

Tools
Global Changes...
Convert Data...
Upgrade Program
Period End ▶
Options...

Clear Audit Trail...
Month End...
Year End...

4 Click on Year End.

5 Click here to update your budget figures for each nominal ledger profit and loss account with the actual values from the year just ending.

Year End

WARNING
This option will change your Financial Year and transfer balances from all Profit and Loss accounts to Retained Earnings.

You should ensure you have taken at least two backup copies of your data prior to running this routine.

Period
Year End Date: 31st December1999
Current Date   31st December1999

Budgets
Transfer Actuals to Budgets   ☐
Percentage Increase   0.00

Postings
Year End Journals:
31/12/1999

Output To
◉ Printer
○ File

OK   Cancel

6 Change Year End Journals Date if necessary.

7 Select Output.

8 Click OK to run.

Lastly, remove any unwanted Customer, Supplier, Nominal, Bank and Product records and reset the date. You are now ready to enter transactions for the new financial year.

Clearing the Audit Trail

Only paid, allocated and reconciled transactions are removed from the Audit Trail.

This option lets you remove paid and reconciled transactions prior to a specified date from the Audit Trail. This makes the ledgers easier to read. Reconciled transactions on the nominal ledger are brought forward as opening balances.

Sage Instant Accounting can store up to 2,000,000,000 transactions in the Audit Trail, so transactions do not always have to be removed. However, by deleting unwanted transactions, this will free disk space and provide faster access to information.

The VAT and Bank columns must display the reconciled flag R to be removed from the Audit Trail.

Only those transactions which have been reconciled for both VAT and the bank can be cleared from the Audit Trail. Therefore, if you find that some transactions are not cleared when you run the Clear Audit Trail function, check the Bank and VAT columns of these transactions in the Audit Trail to see if they are flagged as 'R' for reconciled.

If a transaction on the Audit Trail has a hyphen (-) as a flag in either the Bank or VAT column, this means that bank reconciliation or VAT reconciliation is not applicable for that transaction.

To clear the Audit Trail simply do the following:

| From the Tools menu, select Period End and click Clear Audit Trail.

Department-mental reporting and activity will be effected by removing transactions from the Audit Trail.

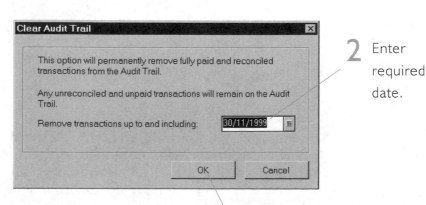

2 Enter required date.

3 Click OK to clear the Audit Trail.

Remember that the Audit Trail is where Sage Instant Accounting stores all of the transactions that you enter. It is so called because it is a complete record of your transaction activities and is often requested by auditors during their investigations.

When you clear transactions from the Audit Trail, the details are removed but the balances they contained are kept and carried forward as opening balances so that your financial reports are all still accurate and up-to-date.

How often you clear down your Audit Trail is up to you and depends on just how many transactions you enter per month. However, the more transactions you leave on the system, the longer it takes Sage Instant Accounting to sort through the list and calculate any values needed for its reports.

Clearing your Audit Trail has the following effect:

- All transactions which are fully paid, allocated and reconciled are permanently removed from the Audit Trail.

- All unreconciled and unallocated supplier and customer transactions which are dated before the date you specified are now brought forward as outstanding items.

Before you do clear the Audit Trail, it is always recommended that you first take a backup and print out a copy of it.

- Any supplier and customer transactions which are dated after the date you specified are now carried forward as outstanding items.

- All unreconciled transactions on the Nominal Ledger will be brought forward as outstanding items.

- The value of all reconciled transactions that have been removed from the Audit Trail appear as an opening balance on each nominal ledger account history.

- Any outstanding or unallocated transactions which are dated before the Clear Audit Trail date you entered, i.e., they are unreconciled or have not yet been paid, are not affected by the Clear Audit Trail function.

The Task Manager

This chapter shows you how to use the Task Manager for setting up useful functions such as a reminder list of tasks to do, i.e., bills to pay, people to contact, etc. It also lets you quickly view the status of your accounts and invoices as well as checking how much you owe and vice versa.

Covers

Chapter Fourteen

Features of the Tasks Option

Why not set up the Task Manager to run whenever you switch your computer on and show a list of invoices due for payment by you or to you that day.

Use the Tasks option to set up a list of jobs that you need to do and to prompt you of any tasks that are currently due, overdue or recently completed. By setting up these tasks it acts as a reminder of the actions you need to take to run your business efficiently, produces important information and saves valuable time.

In brief, the Task Manager helps you run your business by reminding you about the tasks you need to complete as they become due.

You can use the Tasks option to help you:

- Set up a list of tasks that you need to do and also view any tasks that are either completed, due or overdue.

Don't forget to regularly 'tidy up' the To Do entries by removing unwanted tasks from the Completed Tasks list.

- Record the bills you receive and quickly view a list of bills that are paid, those due for payment or any that are overdue.

- Check how much you owe your suppliers and, more important, find out how much you are owed by your customers.

- Check the account status of your customers and suppliers. For example, you will be able to see at a glance which accounts are over the credit limit, inactive or on-hold.

From the Company Stack you can view the company information you entered either in the Startup Wizard or in the Company Preferences option from the Sage Instant Accounting Settings menu.

- View and keep track of any recurring entries you have set up in Sage Instant Accounting. This is particularly useful as it is all too easy to overlook processing your recurring entries at the end of what may turn out to be a very busy month!

- Quickly check the status of your product and service invoices. You may, for example, want to see which invoices or credit notes are due for printing or which have yet to be posted.

The Task Manager can be set up so that it runs when you switch your computer on, hence acting as a useful prompt.

The Task Manager Desktop

 The Application toolbar contains different options with different functions, depending upon the Tasks chosen from the Stacked toolbar.

Your Instant Accounting Task Manager desktop features a menu bar, a stacked toolbar, an application toolbar and a split screen, with tree view on the left and list view on the right.

From the desktop you can set up tasks, remind yourself of jobs to do etc. To bring up the desktop do the following:

1 From the Sage Instant Accounting toolbar, click on the Tasks button.

2 The Menu Bar provides a list of options using drop-down menus.

3 The stacked toolbar area.

4 List View area.

 Options available from the Application toolbar are also available from the Tasks menu. These include New, Open, Delete, Pay and Properties.

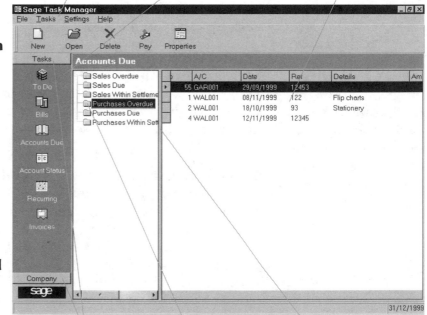

 Use the List View screen (right hand side of the screen) as a shortcut to your tasks, transactions, bills, recurring entries etc. by simply double-clicking on the required entry.

5 Click on the Tasks or Company buttons for the respective toolbars.

6 Select a folder in the Tree View area to bring up a list.

7 Resize the View areas by dragging from here.

You can also access Company details by clicking on Settings, then Company Details from the menu bar.

Task Manager Features

The Task Manager window consists of the following:

The Menu Bar

Clicking with your mouse on each option on the menu bar provides access to a drop-down menu.

The Stacked Toolbar

This toolbar is located vertically down the left side of the Task Manager desktop and contains buttons for the main program options. There are two stacked toolbars available, for Tasks and Company. Switching between the two is easily accomplished by clicking on the buttons marked Tasks and Company respectively.

All of the options on the Tasks stacked toolbar are also available from the drop-down menu that appears when you click on Tasks on the menu bar.

Use the Help facility from the menu bar to aid familiarising yourself with how to use the Task Manager efficiently.

Applications Toolbar

Located across the top of the Task Manager window and just below the menu bar is the Applications toolbar. The buttons on this toolbar perform the appropriate function depending on the option you choose from the Tasks stacked toolbar.

For example, when you choose the Bills option from the stacked toolbar, the New button on the Applications menu allows you to create a new bill. On choosing the To Do option, you can create a new To Do task with the New button. However, the New button is inactive when you choose any of the other options on the stacked toolbar as it is not required. The other buttons on the Applications toolbar also work as appropriate to the selected stacked toolbar option.

The left side of the Desktop screen is the Tree View, the right side is the List View.

The options on the Applications toolbar are also available from the drop-down menu when you click on File on the menu bar.

Click in the List View part of the window with the right mouse button to bring up a list of options for working with your tasks or bills, such as New, Open, Delete etc.

You can resize the Tree and List view columns by simply positioning the mouse cursor on the vertical column divider in the middle of the screen and dragging left or right to the desired size.

The options available from the Tasks menu are also available from the Applications toolbar.

The Tree View

The main viewing area of the Task Manager desktop is divided into two. On the left side is the tree view, so called because is shows the folders available for the option you have chosen from the Tasks stacked toolbar, such as Invoices to Print, Sales Overdue, Overdue Bills or Current Tasks.

If you work with Microsoft Windows, you will be familiar with the tree view.

The List View

On the right side of the viewing area is the list view. When you select a folder for a particular category from the tree view, e.g., Current Tasks, the List view displays the relevant tasks that you have set up.

As you choose different folders in the tree view, the list view changes to show only those items which match that criteria. For example, when you select the Current Bills folder, only those bills that are current are displayed in the list box.

When you pay the bill, the Task Manager recognises the changed status and the bill no longer appears in the list view for current bill. If you now select the Paid Bills folder from the tree view, you will notice that the paid bill now appears in this list, as it now matches a different criteria.

These options within the Task Manager are very useful when you need to quickly refer back to transactions you have completed, such as paid bills. You can see at a glance from the list view if the bill has been paid, or if for some reason it has been overlooked.

Double clicking on a particular entry in the list view brings up the item's properties. In the case of a bill it brings up the bill record, from which you can check the various details you need, such as the amount and date of the bill, the date due and the date the bill was paid. If the bill has only been part paid, the outstanding amount is shown.

Setting up a To Do task

Use the shortcut key CTRL+N, or click the right hand mouse button and select New from the popup menu to set up a new To Do task.

If the Task Complete box is selected, the task is moved from the Current Tasks or Overdue Tasks list to the Complete Tasks list.

When you save your task it appears in the Current Tasks folder on the To Do List.

To delete a task, highlight it from the Current, Overdue, or Completed Tasks and click Delete from the File menu.

Use the To Do option to create a list of tasks you need to complete. The type of tasks include a General Reminder, Send overdue letters, Print management reports etc. Any additional information that may prove useful can be entered within the Description and Notes boxes.

Once saved, the task appears in the Current Tasks folder on the To Do list. This list can then be viewed at any time. To set up a To Do task, proceed as follows:

1 From the Task Manager, click on the To Do option from the Tasks stacked toolbar.

2 Click New from the application toolbar.

4 Enter date when task is due for completion.

3 Select the reminder type from the drop down list box.

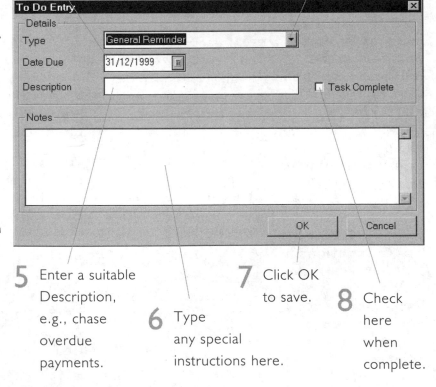

5 Enter a suitable Description, e.g., chase overdue payments.

6 Type any special instructions here.

7 Click OK to save.

8 Check here when complete.

Recording a new Bill

 When the bill details are saved, it will appear in the Current Bills folder on the Bills list. If required you can edit your bill details.

The Bills option provides a useful and convenient way of recording all your bills, such as rates, rent, etc. Once the payment information is entered and saved, the bill will appear in the Current Bills folder on the Bills list. These details can be edited if required at this stage.

Use the Task Manager then to quickly view which bills are paid, due or overdue. To record a new bill:

1 Using Task Manager, click on the Bills option from the Tasks stacked toolbar.

2 Click New from the File menu.

 Once the Bills option has been selected from the Tasks stacked toolbar, you can use the shortcut key CTRL+N to record a new bill.

3 Enter the nominal code for paying the bill to, e.g., if paying your telephone bill the default nominal ledger account is 7502.

4 Describe your transaction here.

 References entered into the Ref box will appear in the Audit Trail for cross referencing purposes.

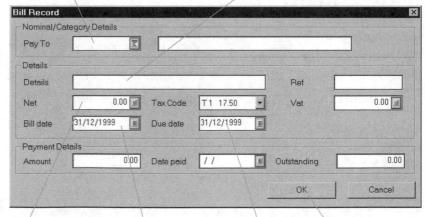

 If a bill is not paid by the Due Date entered, the task is moved to the Overdue Bills folder.

5 Enter Net amount of the bill here.

6 Enter date bill received.

7 Enter date bill is due to be paid.

8 Check all Details and click OK to save.

Paying a Bill

After paying a selected bill, it is moved from the Current Bills or Overdue Bills folder to the Paid Bills folder. The bill payment details are updated on the Bill Record.

Use the Pay option to quickly and easily pay any current/outstanding bills which have been previously set up using Task Manager. To action bill payment the only detail required is the Bank Account nominal code you want to pay the bill from, as follows:

1 Select Bills from the Tasks stacked toolbar.

2 Select either Current Bills or Overdue Bills folder from the Tree view.

3 Select the bill required from the List View.

4 Click the Pay option from the application toolbar.

An alternative way to pay a bill is by clicking the right mouse button, then selecting the Pay option from the popup menu.

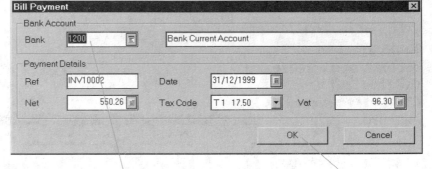

5 Enter nominal code of Bank account to pay bill from.

6 Click OK to pay bill.

If you accidentally try to Pay a bill which has already been paid, Sage Instant Accounting will remind you that there is no outstanding amount to make a payment against.

7 The bill is now paid and moves into the Paid Bills folder.

8 Click on the Paid Bills folder and double-click on the bill you have just paid.

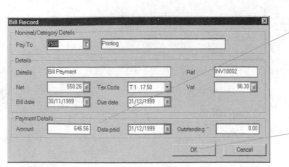

9 Note Record is updated to show payment details.

10 Click OK to close.

Accounts Due

To view more details about a transaction, select the transaction and use shortcut key ALT+ENTER.

Use the Phone button to automatically dial your customer telephone number. Your computer (with modem) needs to share the same line as your telephone.

To view details of different transactions on the list, click the First, Previous, Next or Last buttons.

For a printout of debtors refer to the Customers Reports window.

Use the Accounts Due option from the Tasks stack to identify who owes you money, i.e., Sales Overdue, Sales Due and Sales Within Settlement. If your computer is fitted with a modem you can even get Sage Instant Accounting to dial the customer for you.

To find out which customers owe you money

1 From the Tasks stacked toolbar, select Accounts Due and click the Sales Overdue folder.

2 Note transaction list of overdue payments.

3 For more details, select a transaction.

4 Click Properties from the application toolbar.

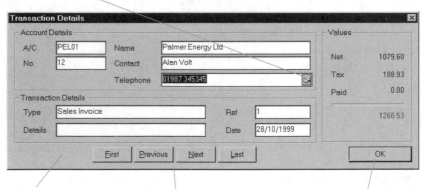

5 The Transaction Details window appears.

6 Use these buttons to move between different transactions in the list.

7 When finished click OK.

...cont'd

Clicking on Purchases Due shows a list of all purchase transactions due for payment today.

To find out who you owe money to

You can also use the Accounts Due option to keep track of who you owe money to, i.e., Purchases Overdue, Purchases Due and Purchases Within Settlement. As with your debtors, provided you entered a telephone number and your computer has a modem, you can ring your Supplier at the click of a button.

1 From the Tasks stacked toolbar, select Accounts Due and click the Purchases Overdue folder.

2 Note transaction list of overdue payments.

The Purchases Overdue folder contains all the purchase transactions you have not paid within the supplier's settlement terms.

3 For more details, select a transaction.

4 Click Properties from the application toolbar.

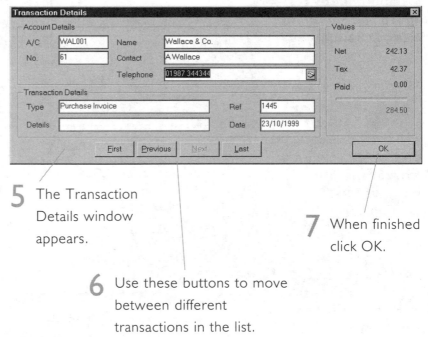

You can also view detailed transaction information by selecting a transaction and clicking the right mouse button, then choosing Properties from the popup menu.

5 The Transaction Details window appears.

7 When finished click OK.

6 Use these buttons to move between different transactions in the list.

Account Status

The Account Status option lets you view accounts that match certain criteria, for example, Sales Over Credit Limit, Sales On Hold, Purchase Over Credit Limit or Purchase On Hold. If you require more detailed information about a transaction, select it and click the Properties button from the application toolbar.

 Use the shortcut key ALT+ ENTER to view transaction properties.

1 From the Instant Accounting Task Manager window, choose the Account Status option from the Tasks stacked toolbar.

2 Select the folder you require from the Tree View list.

 In the Account Details window use the First, Previous, Next and Last buttons to move between different account transactions.

3 Highlight the required account from the List view.

4 Click the Properties button on the application toolbar.

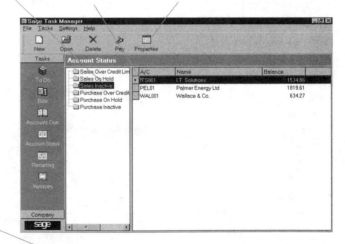

 Use the telephone button to let Sage Instant Accounting dial a customer for you when you want to speak to them about their account.

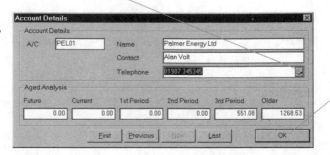

5 When finished, click OK to exit.

The Recurring Option

Using the Task Manager you can view any recurring entries you have set for various transaction types, namely Receipt, Payment, Journal Debit or Journal Credit.

To set up recurring entries select the Recurring option from the Bank toolbar.

You can view the individual details about the transactions, but you cannot change these details. To view details about a recurring payment you set up in Sage Instant Accounting, do the following:

1 From the Sage Task Manager window, choose the Recurring option from the Tasks stacked toolbar.

2 Select the folder you require from the Tree view list, e.g., Payments.

You cannot change your recurring entry details from within the Task Manager.

3 Highlight the required payment from the List view.

4 Click the Properties button on the application toolbar.

5 The details appear for the selected recurring entry.

For detailed information about recurring entries, select transaction and choose the Properties option from the application toolbar.

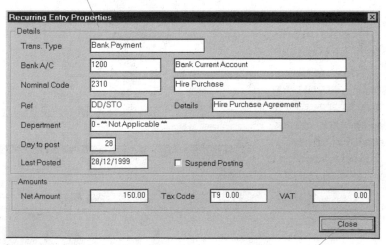

6 Click Close when finished.

Invoices Option

An alternative way to view your invoices is to select Tasks from the Task Manager menu bar and click Invoices.

Within Task Manager you can view the status of any invoices or credit notes that you have recorded.

Invoices and credit notes are listed separately depending on whether they have been printed or posted. You can also quickly view which invoices or credit notes need printing or posting.

For example, do the following to quickly view a list of invoices which you have not yet printed:

1 From the Sage Task Manager window, click on the Invoices option.

To print/ post an invoice or credit note or record an invoice/credit note number, return to the Invoicing option on the Sage Instant Accounting toolbar then select your transaction and use the Print option.

2 Select the Inv to Print folder.

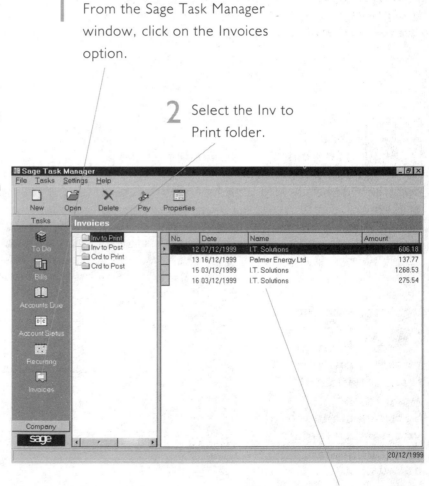

Properties function is not available when viewing invoices or credit notes in the Task Manager.

3 A list of invoices not yet printed appears.

The Company Stack

This feature is useful for quickly viewing your Company Details, such as Name, Address, Telephone, Fax, VAT Reg. No., Web Site and E-mail.

You can also select Company Details from the Settings menu on the Sage Instant Accounting Task Manager toolbar to view your Company Details.

These details, however, cannot be edited using this screen. To do so you will need to exit from the Task Manager and return to Sage Instant Accounting. Then, select Company Preferences from the Instant Accounting Settings menu and make your changes using the Address tab. See Page 21.

To quickly view Company Details from the Task manager just do the following:

1 Click on the Company button at the foot of the stacked toolbar.

You cannot edit your company's details in Task Manager.

2 Click on Company Details to view information.

Use the Company Preferences option from the Instant Accounting Settings menu when you need to update your company details.

3 The Details window appears.

4 Click OK to close.

Hints and Shortcuts

In this chapter you will learn how to set up other useful defaults, record memos and place a customer account on hold, as well as quick ways of performing some of the more common and regular Sage Instant Accounting functions. It introduces you to the predefined shortcut keys provided by Instant Accounting and also shows you the fast ways of navigating through various tasks necessary for running your business efficiently.

Covers

Chapter Fifteen

Customer Record Defaults

You will need to enter such details as credit limit, discount, department, etc., each time you create a new customer record. Use the Customer Defaults option to let Sage Instant Accounting do this for you automatically.

When you create a new customer account, Sage Instant Accounting gives the customer several default settings automatically. These include default codes for transactions entered for this customer, such as nominal ledger code, tax code, currency and department, etc.

These default settings are taken from those you entered as the main Customer Defaults from the Settings menu. If desired, you can then specifically adjust these settings from the Defaults tab on an individual customer record.

If these default settings do not apply to a certain record, you can also set up a customer's defaults for an individual customer record.

To set up your Customer Record Defaults

You can quickly set up Customer defaults as follows:

Use the same procedure for setting up defaults for your suppliers, after clicking on Supplier Defaults from the Settings menu.

1 From the Instant Accounting Settings menu, choose Customer Defaults.

2 Enter the Credit Limit you give your customers. Sage will warn you when a customer exceeds this.

3 If you offer a discount for early or on time payment, enter it here.

Any defaults copied into your new invoices or customer records can always be edited manually if need be.

4 Enter terms here. This can be printed on your statement or invoice.

5 Enter default Tax Code and N/C to be used for new invoices and customer records.

6 Click OK.

Customer Memos

You can also set up a memo for your suppliers. Follow this same procedure after clicking on Suppliers from the Instant Accounting toolbar.

You can record readily available notes about each of your customers through the Memo tab in the Customer Record window.

For example, you may wish to make a note of the date and times you talk or write to your customers, or you could enter some reminder notes to tell them about special new products or special price offers you have.

Each memo is stored as a text file and uses the customer account reference as its filename. These text files can then be loaded into most text processors or other Windows applications for printing, or incorporating into letters or reports.

Sage Instant Accounting allows you to enter up to 800 lines of text in a single memo! To set up a memo:

You can also bring up the Customer Record window by double-clicking on any customer record.

| From the Customers window, select the record you want and click on the Record button.

2 Click on the Memo tab.

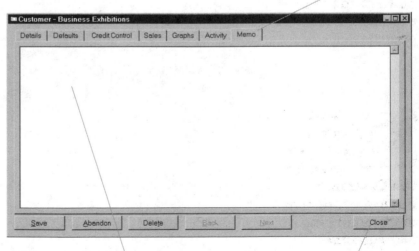

If you make a mistake whilst setting up a memo, simply click on the Abandon button and start again.

3 Type or edit text as you wish. Sage Instant Accounting will automatically wrap text onto the next line as appropriate.

4 When finished, click Close to save the memo.

Putting a Customer's Account On Hold

.Sage Instant Accounting only issues you a warning that the account is on hold. You will still be able to process transactions.

Occasionally, if you are having problems with a customer, you may need to place their account on hold so that you can have the situation flagged to you before processing future orders.

Sage Instant Accounting allows you to do this easily. Then, each time you attempt to process a transaction for that customer, Instant Accounting will bring the account status to your attention.

To place a customer's account on hold, do the following:

Use Account Status from Task Manager, Sales On Hold folder to provide you with an up to date list of customer accounts on hold.

1 Select the Customers button from the Sage Instant Accounting toolbar.

2 Highlight the customer record required and click on the Record button.

3 Select the Credit Control tab.

Remember that you can also bring up the Customer Record window by double-clicking on any customer record.

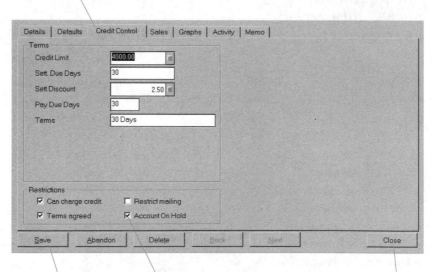

4 Click here to place the Account On Hold.

5 Click Save to record the change.

6 Click Close.

Hidden Hotkeys

Use the Hotkeys as often as you can to make using Sage Instant Accounting quicker and easier. The more you use them, the less time it will take you to perform certain regular actions.

Sage Instant Accounting provides you with a number of shortcut functions to make using the program easier. As you become familiar with Instant Accounting, you should try to make use of these shortcuts as it will speed up the time it takes you to enter or process transactions.

All of the functions listed below are termed Hidden Hotkeys, because you simply hold down the control key on your keyboard as you press a second appropriate key to perform a function that you would normally have to go through one of the menu options with the mouse cursor for.

The Hidden Hotkeys in Sage Instant Accounting are:

Before using some of the Hotkeys, such as Bold, Cut, Copy and Underline, etc., you must first have selected a section of text to perform the action on.

- CTRL+A   Selects all
- CTRL+B   This shortcut makes selected text appear in Bold
- CTRL+C   Copies selected text
- CTRL+I   Change selected text to Italic
- CTRL+N   New
- CTRL+O   Open
- CTRL+P   Print
- CTRL+S   Save
- CTRL+U   Underline selected text
- CTRL+V   Paste text or object previously copied
- CTRL+X   Cut selected text
- CTRL+Z   Undo the last action

Click Help on the Sage Instant Accounting menu bar to bring up a diagram of the available shortcut keys. Click on the diagram to close it.

- CTRL+ LEFT MOUSE BUTTON   From the grey margin, highlights all the objects across the line.

Command Buttons

 Use the command buttons regularly to make data entry easier.

To make data entry easier, Instant Accounting provides you with a range of buttons specific to certain boxes:

The Finder Button

Used on all text boxes which require a record code entry. Clicking on this button brings up a list of available account codes to choose from.

 So that you can become familiar with using Sage Instant Accounting without altering your own data, you are provided with a set of demo data to practice on. Click on File from the Sage Instant Accounting menu and select Open Demo Data to access it. To return to your own data, click on File again and select Open Instant Data.

The Calendar Button

All date text boxes have a Calendar button attached to make date selection easier.

The Calculator Button

This is attached to most numeric data entry boxes. Click on this button to display a mini-calculator to help you enter values.

The Opening Balances Button

Click on this button when entering opening balances for each customer, supplier, nominal ledger and bank account record.

The Edit Button

Use the Edit Button when you need to enter special one-off details, such as discounts to be applied, changes to the unit price and comments, against items on product and service invoices and credit notes.

 Use the Demo Data to practice entering certain transactions you are unfamiliar with – that is what it is there for!

The Dial Button

Simply click on the dial button to have Sage Instant Accounting phone or fax your customers and suppliers for you. You can also use it to launch a Web site or to send e-mail to your clients.

Once you have found your way around Sage Instant Accounting, you should have become familiar with the above buttons and their uses. Use them regularly to save time.

Index